The Entrepreneur's Playbook

WHY NOT YOU!

50 Years of Wisdom for Business Success

CHRISTOPHER W. KURZ

To Debbie....

Contents

Foreword 7

Preface.. 9

Introduction.. 11

Chapter 1 15
The Four Keys to Success—Passion, Attitude,
Lifetime Learning, and Pearls of Wisdom

Chapter 2.. 25
Personal Risks, Enterprise Risk Management,
and Risks You Can Not Control: Stress Management

Chapter 3 41
Lawyers, Accountants, and Consultants: Business Necessities

Chapter 4.. 45
Marketing: What are You Really Selling?

Chapter 5.. 71
Demographics, Statistical Analysis, and Your Gut

Chapter 6.. 77
Finance: The Unfortunate Necessity of Other Peoples' Money

Chapter 7.. 89
Business Analytics: The KISS Principle

Chapter 8.. 97
Personnel: Employees Are Smart. Listen to Them.

Chapter 9 113
Business Strategies and Culture

Chapter 10 131
Mega Trends: Sustainability and Diversity, Equity, and Inclusion

Chapter 11 141
Succession: The Queen is Dead. Long Live the King.

Contents

Conclusion 151

Acknowledgements 155

Appendix 157

Christopher W. Kurz

Foreword

By Bob Nillson
Founder, 100 Entrepreneurs Foundation

Having been in business for over 60 years and been an ardent reader of everything I could find that helped explain to me how entrepreneurship worked, I started reading *WHY NOT YOU!* expecting more of the same, overly complicated explanations using a vocabulary that I had to keep a dictionary nearby to understand.

Imagine my pleasant surprise when I found a source I could not put down of brilliant common-sense ideas, pearls of wisdom, the importance of luck, and the importance of time in the trenches. I was infatuated with what I was reading, could not help but compare the author's learning curve to my own, and mostly kept thinking, why didn't I see this 50 years ago.

When I started in business, I was a recent Civil Engineer graduate from Rensselaer Polytechnic Institute, a Marine veteran, including a tour in Vietnam, an eye opener, and thought I knew quite a bit about everything. Little did I know. I couldn't even spell entrepreneurship. One of my first jobs after the Marines was working for real estate developers. I had no clue how real estate deals came together, much less the roles of contractor/ developer/ designers/ and bankers. Where was this book then?

What I really liked, and I've known Chris for over 20 years through working together as members of the Urban Land Institute, is he lays out his learning curve like a road map or WAZE map, in terms that I can understand while integrating the efforts of thinking, ingenuity, creativity, overlayed with banking, finance, legal issues, personnel, and ethics without ever using the word. He also mentions the importance of luck, which I learned in Vietnam is of major importance. Luck can have a huge impact on your business, both positive and negative.

You will learn from the beginning that passion is a key ingredient of what Chris does and I strongly believe what makes the successful entrepreneurs I've known have the successes they have had.

This is a must read for those entering the business world and an important refresher for those that are entrepreneurs and trying to figure out what next trick to use that will give them an edge. For myself in the real estate industry and as the founder of 100 Entrepreneurs, I have met some of the most outstanding businessmen and women that constantly follow the sharing of experience as a guiding principal in their business practice. This is truly an example of learning "How to."

We need more of this as we continue to learn throughout our lifetime.

Read and enjoy,
Bob Nilsson
Founder, 100 Entrepreneurs Foundation

Preface

Becoming a successful entrepreneur has traditionally been a long-term exercise marred by trial and error. Too often, the error comes after it is too late. In the early years of your business life, there is simply not enough experience to avoid the downs and capitalize on the ups. If you are very fortunate, an entrepreneurial mentor will guide you away from errors and toward success.

It would have been very nice to have such a mentor. Having grown up in a family that was not in business, I had no one to ask or to lean on when tough decisions had to be made.

This book is born out of the hope that, from it, you will have a mentor to point you toward the right and sidestep the wrong.

Looking back over my fifty years as an entrepreneur, I realized that having certain personal traits became keys to my success. There is no guarantee of success just for having these traits, but they did tend to tilt the playing field in the right direction. While I never had an entrepreneurial mentor, there were a series of older, wiser men and women who occasionally said or did something worth remembering. Those words became Pearls of Wisdom.

Somehow, some way, things fell into place for me. My career emerged, I grasped opportunities, and eventually, success followed. Not directly, but eventually. At some point, the pieces coalesced. A pattern evolved. There was this attitude, coupled with passion, more education, and exposure to older (and sometimes younger), wiser people. All these things created success.

Is this what happens to other successful people? How do they find out about the pieces? Is this unique to entrepreneurs?

Over the years, especially when the gray hair came, business friends asked me if I could mentor their daughter or son. Organizations wanted me to mentor their participants, who, after I mentored them, all asked why I did not teach.

The answer was, "No time." Business and my family took all the available time. The best I could do was be a guest lecturer at Harvard, the Wharton School at the University of Pennsylvania, local universities, and Urban Land Institute meetings.

The aha moment was that maybe writing a book as a guide to being a successful entrepreneur might help more people, and faster. I casually mentioned the idea to several friends, and their collective response was. "You need to do this." WHY NOT YOU. So, I did.

Several friends with experience in writing and publishing stepped in and opened the doors to the book-writing world. When asked, those who have written books were generous with their time when talking about going from an idea to a published tome.

My wish is that you find this book helpful and entertaining, and that you occasionally refer to it for Pearls of Wisdom and WHY NOT ME inspiration.

Christopher W. Kurz

Introduction

There are many books written by Fortune 500 CEOs who espouse their management styles, and reasons for their success. Academics have also written many books about the philosophies and principles of being a successful entrepreneur.

This book is neither. This book is based on the trials and tribulations, mistakes made, and lessons learned by a successful entrepreneur starting from the ground up. From the "trenches," so to speak. The book is a guide to becoming a successful entrepreneur and leader in the field of your passion.

This book starts with four Keys to Success and then dives into the key elements of business: Risk, Finance, Marketing, Personnel, Business Analytics, and Mega Business Strategies. It ends, appropriately, with Succession.

Each element includes the basics, illustrated by anecdotes drawn from my business experience and that of others.

Successful entrepreneurship is a combination of these four Keys to Success: Passion, Attitude (referred to as WHY NOT ME or WNM's), a commitment to Lifetime Learning, and the accumulation of Pearls of Wisdom (PW's) from your own experiences and those of others. Hopefully, these topics and related business stories in this book will help you become the successful leader and entrepreneur you want to be. These stories are not all about rocket shots directly to success. There are ups, downs, good times, and bad. The trajectory is more like a scatter diagram that eventually ends with success. The stories in this book are intended to illustrate moments of passion and attitude, refined by Pearls of Wisdom and a lifetime of learning. There are over thirty-two Pearls of Wisdom and eleven WHY NOT ME moments in the book.

It starts with Passion. If you are passionate about something, you rise every morning eager to work. You may make a lot of money or may not make much money, but you will be happy. If you are not passionate about your work, at the end of the day, there is no amount of money that somebody can pay you to make you happy.

Attitude is the elixir that, when stirred with passion, creates the environment for a successful entrepreneur. It is a WHY NOT ME attitude that makes the difference. Added to this mix are Pearls of Wisdom. Throughout your life, you have experiences that resonate and become a part of your being. The important thing is to remember these experiences, take them to heart, and learn from them. Some are immediately important. Some take time to marinate and reveal themselves down the road. Some are readily apparent, and others only emerge years later, but they shape the passion and the attitude and help refine and improve your business.

Education does not stop with the last university degree. Your industry is constantly changing. It is vital to stay educated on the latest trends, technologies, and changes happening in your field of interest. Commit to a lifetime of learning, of educating yourself over and over.

My Passion turned out to be creating and building things. This manifested itself first in commercial real estate development and later in finance and banking. Some, but not all of all the stories in this book come from real estate. For those interested, there is an Appendix with a list of real estate projects featured in this book. Lessons learned from real estate stories have been translated to general business so that the Pearls of Wisdom resonate with you wherever your passions lie.

The Four Keys to Success are relevant to all businesses, not just real estate. In each chapter, Pearls of Wisdom are highlighted with this symbol.

This book is, in part, based on my career in commercial real estate and finance. There were career stops in banking, mortgage banking, and investment banking. For context, it is helpful to know that my first real job experience was as an employee at The Rouse Company, a developer of regional malls and new towns. The first entrepreneurial company was The McGill Development Company with Peter McGill, and the second was Linden Associates, Inc., wholly owned. The real estate projects that these stories draw from are, in chronological order: Sherway Gardens at Rouse, Columbia Business Center, Columbia Corporate Park (AT&T), and Bel Air Town Center at McGill, and the Horse Farm, and Arundel Mills Corporate Park at Linden.

My first job working at a bank included car leasing, credit cards, consumer banking, real estate workouts, and mortgage banking. Later, three of us started the Columbia Bank, a community bank that grew into a billion-dollar enterprise. It was more fun being at the top of that bank than toward the bottom the first time around. After working at the first bank, I spent three years running the Baltimore office of a mortgage banking company, and five years at an investment bank doing primarily real estate investing.

From then on, it was 100 percent entrepreneur—the good and the bad, the ups and the downs.

CHAPTER 1

The Four Keys to Success: Passion, Attitude, Lifetime Learning, and Pearls of Wisdom

PASSION

When someone says they are passionate about something, what does that mean to you? The dictionary definition is "showing, or caused by, strong feelings or a strong belief."

In this book, it is more of an "I can't get enough of this," or "I could do this all day long." The subject matter just gives you immense interest and satisfaction. The more of it you have, the more you want. Your passion may not be like that, but it will be something you are interested in and enjoy doing. It may not come on quickly, and its reasons may change over time. As a kid, I was always drawn to the house blueprints in my mom's *House Beautiful* magazine. A summer job exposed the complexity of real estate and its ability to satisfy basic human needs. A second summer job sucked me in all the way. Your passion will, no doubt, be different and unique to you.

WHY NOT ME (ATTITUDE)

Attitude is a developed skill. Sometimes it is intentional, and sometimes it is out of desperation. Eventually, it becomes a part of your personality. My first attitude change, WHY NOT ME moment, came out of desperation after the first semester of my sophomore year in college.

One of the great things about going to college is that your freshman year starts with a blank slate. Unless you are going to the local state university, there probably are no existing friends. You can be whoever you want to be for four years. At the end of four years, you graduate with a diploma, a GPA, a major, and lots of memories. Everything else that happens during the college years does not become baggage to be carried for the rest of your life. College is a truly remarkable opportunity to explore new things and test yourself, knowing that failure will not be permanent.

That first fall, there was a group of upperclassmen gathered around three rowing oars tied at the top to form a tripod. They were recruiting freshmen for the lightweight crew. Growing up as a late bloomer, I was never big enough to play or excel at football, basketball, or baseball. Having physically caught up, rowing looked like a great opportunity. How many other people already knew how to row? How hard could it be? This decision proved to be one of my most transformative decisions in college. Although unknown at the time, it was the very first of my WHY NOT ME decisions, a positive, you-can-do-this attitude. There were about seventy-five other freshmen who went out for the lightweight crew. By spring, this group had pared to approximately twenty. I was fortunate enough to earn a spot in the first freshman boat.

It was a wonderful, gratifying experience. It was the first time in my life that I tried something completely new—WHY NOT ME. It was the first time working with a group of people, placing the group's success before your own—WHY NOT US. And, we were not just good, we were excellent. Our success resulted from an excellent freshman coach and a belief by the older rowers that the rowing program was improving. Our freshman crew finished the year second in the country and redefined for me what was possible. Why not be the best of the best!

As you grow your company, attitude becomes much more about the company, and about WHY NOT US.

Second-semester freshmen were allowed to join a fraternity. At a large university like Penn, fraternities provided a much smaller group of people to associate with. Just about everybody joined a fraternity.

Freshman year was filled with the excitement of learning how to row and getting to know a group of friends from rowing and the fraternity. Academics were an afterthought. The assumption was that you had learned how to study in high school and that these skills would carry you through your higher education. That proved to be wrong.

Sophomore year started with a bang. Fraternity parties after football games with great bands and beer happened almost every weekend. Rowing was rewarding, as the two Penn Lightweight boats finished first and second at the Head of the Charles Regatta in Boston.

Toward the end of the semester, the academic wheels began to fall off the cart. First-semester sophomore grades were two Bs, one C, and two Ds. Hoping to be a math major but flunking the course on set theory, the professor suggested that there would be no future for me as a math major. Having not missed a class, the professor awarded a D. The English course turned out to be the course that the English department used to weed English majors from those who should not be English majors. Never having wanted to be an English major, it was a painful awakening.

The status quo was not working. My approach to academics that I learned in high school was not at all suited for the college world. Something had to change. It was time to assess what was, and was not, happening. What had always worked no longer did. Something had to change—lots had to change. But what and how? After a month of introspection and reassessment, I concluded that I required a significant attitude adjustment.

The result of this adjustment was WHY NOT ME. Everything was up for change. It was necessary to believe that change could happen, was possible, and could lead to great outcomes. If you want to get good grades, you must first believe that you are entitled to good grades.

Out went reading textbooks and underlining important passages in yellow magic marker. Out went sitting in the back of the classroom and not asking questions. I now took written notes on everything I read, replacing the yellow magic marker. The seat in the back of the classroom became the middle seat in the front row. One serious question must be asked of the professor in every class. Professor office hours were mandatory.

I only realized years later that this metamorphosis could be summed up in three words "WHY NOT ME." It was the value of assessing the present and recalibrating for the future. There were no guarantees this was going to work, but it was clear that repeating the same old, same old was not going to work.

Over the second semester of sophomore year and the beginning of junior year, these changes began to bear fruit. My grades improved. My relationships with professors became important and rewarding. No more Math classes and no more English classes. Economics and Art History proved interesting.

Liking Economics and wanting to take more courses, I took a trip to the economics department and requested to be put in the honors program. The department said yes! As a political science major, achieving honors involved a review of your coursework and an interview with the department heads. Despite having received a D in freshman-year Introductory Political Science, somehow the interview went well, and honors in political science were granted. I graduated with honors in political science and economics! Two years earlier, this was not even a dream of mine. Part of the WHY NOT ME attitude is to reach for the stars . Less successful was an effort to qualify as a Rhodes Scholar. Nothing ventured, nothing gained. WHY NOT ME is not a guarantee.

LIFETIME LEARNING

One of the characteristics of a successful entrepreneur is a relentless curiosity about almost everything. Why are things the way they are? Why did she do this differently? How might this apply to my business?

Sometimes the venue for this curiosity is formal—a course, lecture, or industry meeting. And sometimes it is very informal—a conversation with a stranger or sitting on a bench and watching consumers. Sometimes it is even a conversation with yourself. Ever notice that people walk on the same side of a sidewalk as they drive on a road? How is the width of that sidewalk reflected in a walker's smile, or lack thereof? When you have a meeting, do you sit facing the windows or with your back to them? Others in the meeting? What does that say about their mood? How does that impact your meeting strategy?

Sometimes it happens early in your career. As a child of a career Navy officer, I had absolutely no exposure to business. No friends with parents in business. My first exposure to the business world was attending graduate business school. My first year in the MBA program at Wharton was an eye-opener. Having received honors in economics as an undergraduate, it seemed reasonable to try and wave out of similar courses for first-year Wharton graduate students. My professors decided that I did not need to repeat macroeconomics, but an exam would be required to waive out of microeconomics. I took the exam, and another semester of microeconomics was deemed necessary. It did not help that I wrote the entire exam spelling profit as "prophet." That's right. It is a miracle I was not immediately expelled.

My first semester at Wharton resulted in a modified form of WHY NOT ME. While the same initial studying criteria were applied, it became immediately clear that, in the business world, things are done differently than in the undergraduate world. This best manifested itself in a market research class. My first paper resulted in a C and a trip to the professor to ask what an A paper was like. He produced a one-page outline written by one of the other students, which contrasted with my five-page dissertation on the question at hand. Dr. Frank pointed out that this was not an English class and that, in the business world, brevity was valued.

Formal continuing education beyond your job is easily put off, but it is necessary to be on the cutting edge of your industry. In real estate, the best group for lifetime learning, in my opinion, is the Urban Land Institute. They have courses to take locally and nationally, but the best place to learn is at their semiannual national meetings. A key part of the ULI culture is that if someone asks you a question, you answer completely and honestly. Early in the development business, we were interested in a new type of office/warehouse building that was gaining popularity in Silicon Valley.

The originator of this building type was spotted at a ULI meeting, and we approached him. His immediate response was, "I have a half hour. Let's sit down now and talk." Wow.

Over the years, ULI has been a source of intentional and unintentional education. Now I go early to the meetings and stay late, minimize appointments, and try to attend sessions on topics I know little about, absorbing information like a sponge. Look for the ULI of your industry. Pick an organization that the industry leaders belong to and has a mission to educate its members.

PEARLS OF WISDOM

Rowing my sophomore year proved to be more difficult. Now demoted to the third boat, there seemed to be no WHY NOT ME attitude adjustment available. Jack, our coach during freshmen year, agreed to a one-on-one session in the tanks.

The tanks are an on-land version of rowing. The oars have holes in them. The rower sits on a slide like in a shell. There are large tubs of water on either side of the slide that the oar moves through. The coach started with a standard warm-up and asked for twenty hard strokes known as a "power twenty" in rowing lingo. Midway through the power twenty, Jack started to yell and scream at me, calling for more effort. Then he said, "Stop, stop, stop. I know exactly what your problem is."

This is what Jack said:

"When a person is under high stress, they tend to rely on their strengths. This is not the right thing to do. When a person is under high stress, they should focus on their weaknesses. Your strengths are probably already good enough for the situation, but improving your weaknesses can truly make the difference."

In the context of rowing, the strength was literally the physical effort. But fast shells are a combination of strength and the rhythm of all eight rowers moving in perfect sync. My weakness was that when God passed out rhythm, I was not in the line.

Jack's advice was that, when called upon for a power twenty, think rhythm, not strength. It made a huge difference.

This was the first great Pearl of Wisdom, an aha moment that had a lasting influence.

PEARL OF WISDOM:
Appreciate your strengths but know your weaknesses. When it is crunch time, focus on the weaknesses.

Jack's advice bore fruit on the water. A month before the spring season of my junior year, the rowing coach determined the first and second boat lineup. I was in the second boat. For the next two weeks, our second boat proceeded to beat the first boat at every distance. A week before the season started, the second boat challenged the first boat to a race to see which crew would be the first boat against Georgetown. We won and the next Saturday we beat Georgetown's first boat. On the following Monday, the coach changed the lineup. The process repeated itself weekly throughout the season. Our poor coach kept changing the lineup only to find out that no one combination of rowers was consistently faster than another. The first two boats were equally fast. Rhythm was hard at work that spring. It was not until years later that I realized that this David-versus-Goliath story would form the entrepreneurial foundation when confronting much larger corporations. It was truly a WHY NOT ME experience. But not as an individual. Rowing is absolutely a team endeavor. This was a WHY NOT US experience. In business, it is almost always WHY NOT US.

In the business world, the parallel to strength and rhythm in rowing, for me, turned out to be analytics and listening. Always good at math, the Excel spreadsheet was a home away from home. Listening and its nuances was my unknown weakness until it raised its ugly head.

Learning to listen is important. Knowing our relative strengths and weaknesses is a big key to success.

The corollary to listening is silence. Knowing when to not say anything can be more impactful than talking. Often, the folks on the other side of the conversation are so eager to talk that they divulge their positions before being asked. Try it.

Sometimes a Pearl of Wisdom comes from yourself. Hopefully, you were listening when you articulated it. I did remember this Pearl of Wisdom.

It is generally believed that real estate developers are against the environment and that environmentalists are against any development. At breakfast with the head of a major national environmental group, I proposed the following hypothesis:

Instead of these two groups being at opposite ends of a very long spectrum with nothing in common, perhaps the two groups were actually standing in the middle of the spectrum with their backs to each other. Perhaps they had much more in common than they realized, and by working together, they both could accomplish far more than when in opposition to each other.

After further discussion, the environmental group joined an alliance of a sister environmental group, the Home Builders of Maryland, and the Urban Land Institute to formulate a series of proposals to the state government to improve the environment, which were supported by the building industry. As important as the proposals were, the friendships formed among the groups made future collaborative efforts much easier and more productive.

PEARL OF WISDOM:
Having different beliefs does not make you enemies. Seeking common ground often gets you farther than being combative.

Risks come with any business. The best you can hope for is that you see them coming and are prepared. Otherwise known as Stress Management.

CHAPTER 2
Personal Risk, Enterprise Risk Management, and Risks Beyond Your Control: Stress Management

PERSONAL RISK

The "elephant in the room" for any aspiring entrepreneur is how to bridge the time between the last paycheck and enough positive cash flow from the new venture to support yourself.

The common perception is that a twice-a-month paycheck is a great source of security. Not so. Somewhere lost in this security blanket is the fact that the employer can lay people off at any time, with or without reason. Employers may or may not offer severance. There may or may not be signs that layoffs are forthcoming. The stark reality is that the financial security of the paycheck is nothing more than a two-week security blanket. This risk may seem low if job performance is high and the company is doing well financially, but regardless, it is there.

The key is to acknowledge and manage this risk, holding on to the paycheck as long as possible, and then making the jump to the dark side. Most often, nascent entrepreneurs work two jobs: the one with the paycheck and the one without. Having a spouse with a good paycheck helps a lot.

Being laid off at The Rouse Company was my wake-up call. The signs were there, the company was in financial trouble, and people had been told layoffs were coming. Nevertheless, when it came, it was a terrible shock. A bank job materialized and became my next job. It led to an exposure to mortgage banking, and eventually a route back into commercial real estate, this time on my own.

In previous WHY NOT ME times, the institution—school or grad school—did not change. It was a known—a rock amid change. This time, the institution was gone. My confidence that had supported prior WHY NOT ME moments was also gone. Adrift, an opportunity arose to do real estate workouts at a local bank. The person who ran that operation was one of the most highly respected real estate professionals in the region. He became a mentor and expanded my knowledge of commercial real estate well beyond regional malls. His group also did mortgage brokerage, which would later become the lifeline and bridge back into commercial real estate development. A year into this new job, the boss said he was negotiating his departure from the bank. There would be opportunities to go either into the real estate or consumer lending departments. His strong advice was to go to the consumer side of the bank because the bank thought I needed to be "reprogrammed" to undo the "harm" he had inflicted on me as a real estate banker.

This immediately became another WHY NOT ME moment. I was completely out of commercial real estate, working in a completely new field with no passion, and in an organization that was as far from being entrepreneurial as possible. It was time to recalibrate and figure out how to get back to the entrepreneurial world where my passion was. Mortgage banking proved to be the vehicle. A chance phone call from an old mortgage banking client led to a conversation with the Travelers real estate folks in Philadelphia. They said the Mid-Atlantic region had been given to a mortgage banking company, HG Smithy, and that Smithy was looking to open a Baltimore office. In a conversation with the

CEO of Smithy, he asked if he could talk with my initial boss at the bank. The next day, the CEO called and offered the job to open the Baltimore office. Later, it would turn out that the Wharton MBA, plus a strong endorsement from my old boss, had led to the job. I was back in an entrepreneurial environment and working in commercial real estate as a mortgage banker, but now humbled by the events of the past several years.

A part of this WHY NOT ME experience led to the realization that if one truly desires to control one's destiny, one should be completely invested in the profession. This meant joining industry professional organizations and getting to know others in the field, especially headhunters. The local Mortgage Bankers Association provided the opportunity for monthly meetings, a once-a-year national meeting, and an avenue to pursue this goal. The result was an article I wrote in the national MBA publication and several speaking engagements at national meetings. My name was getting out.

My first route to the DARK SIDE was the two-job approach. It involved a "paycheck" job in mortgage banking and starting a company with Peter McGill. This would morph into a five-year "paycheck" job at an investment banking firm that agreed to my continued ownership in the new company. When it was time to make the jump, I was lucky that the two-job approach worked as well as it did.

The first order of business was to find office space. A friend offered a temporary office while the Smithy space was being built out. He mentioned the name, Peter McGill, who had been at Rouse in the leasing department. Pete had returned to Baltimore to start his own company. His office suite was complete, and his temporary office was now available for Smithy.

Pete's goals were to expand his regional mall leasing business and to develop local real estate. A friendship evolved. We eventually decided to see what we could do together in the development world. The McGill Development Company was formed, a 50-50 joint venture consisting of the two of us. Smithy blessed the side business, provided there were no conflicts of interest; and a four-acre lot in Columbia, Maryland, was identified for a forty-thousand-square-foot flex building. It was fortunate that Smithy went along with this side business, as it became the first financial bridge—the paycheck to enable building our own business.

Neither of us had a dime. We floundered. It was WHY NOT ME time, a time to recalibrate and try a different approach. Our aha moment was the realization that our skill sets were in our experience and not our financial resources. It was time to focus on this strength and recognize the financial weakness. Thanks again, Jack, for your Pearl of Wisdom.

A financial partner emerged and a local bank was willing to make the construction loan. The project was built and leased. At the end of the day, we made no money, and the financial partner ended up owning the project. But we had started, built, and leased our very first project. It was 1978 and The McGill Development Company was on its way.

The next project was Columbia Business Park, a twenty-acre, 150,000-square-foot mixed-use (office, flex, and retail) project two blocks from the initial building. A major insurance company liked the project, thought the nascent McGill Development Company could perform, and offered to joint venture the project, providing all the money. Pete graciously agreed to move his office to the construction trailer and spent a miserable winter overseeing the project.

Having never taken the risk of being without a paycheck, there was an interim move before taking the plunge. The mortgage banking business continued to prosper, and headhunters began to call. One of the interested parties was a local investment banking firm wanting to start a mortgage brokerage business. While this was not exactly a WHY NOT ME moment, but it was time to think seriously about the future. What if I could increase my paycheck and formalize ownership in McGill? A win-win or so I thought.

One of the downsides of being a real estate person at a bank or investment bank is that there is no career path to the top. The real estate person is the equivalent of the left-handed relief pitcher in baseball, appropriate for very specific situations, but never intended to be one of the key players. Having turned down offers in Kansas City and Denver, I had a pretty good idea of my value in the marketplace.

The local investment bank made an attractive offer. Pete weighed in, saying that time spent at the investment bank could pay big dividends for our development business. As a Baltimore native, he knew of what he spoke. The investment bank was willing to pay market value and agreed that the fifty percent stake in the McGill Development Company could remain. Years later, this would be identified as the defining moment to head towards being a full-time entrepreneur without the safety net of a paycheck. The time with the investment bank became the financial bridge and cushion to make this journey much easier.

The ability to keep the partnership interest in the McGill Development Company was not without cost. While the investment bank had agreed in writing to the retention of my interest in McGill, the growing success of the development company bothered more than a few people at the bank. Typically, men and women who are successful at an investment bank make nice salaries, but have substantial bonuses based on their success. Despite having been successful at the bank with said success being recognized, bonuses were meager. I asked why this was so. The boss said that my involvement with the development company was resented by some. While entitled to a much larger bonus, leadership felt it should be nominal. The boss asked how serious the development company could become. The answer was that if it performed as hoped for, in five years there would be no need to work for a living. He later said that he knew then that it was only a matter of time before I went full-time with McGill Development. He was right.

Not every entrepreneur has an opportunity for this type of bridge into the unknown. When Pete came back to Baltimore, he had the confidence to go out on his own. He had some business lined up, but it was not a five-year financial cushion. Looking back, the decisions about mortgage banking and creating an industry identity were probably the major catalysts enabling this route.

Going back to the session in the rowing tanks with Jack, it became clear that my two major strengths were analytical analysis and marketing. The weaknesses were a complete inability to read people or feel the faint breeze that would become the hurricane. Fortunately, Pete's great strength was his ability to read people and the situation and feel the breeze at the right time.

There came a time when it was opportune for us to buy out the institutional partner of Columbia Business Center. A replacement equity investor and debt financing were lined up. Ten-year spreadsheets were done to determine the market value of the project. In Pete's office on the speakerphone, the call was made to the institutional partner offering to buy them out of the project.

About two minutes into the conversation, Pete writes a note on a scrap piece of paper and passes it over. It says "Do *not* budge on the price."

The initial offered price was substantially below our determination of the fair market value, but the institutional partner agreed to the price during the call.

After the phone call, I immediately asked Pete, "How did you know?" Pete said that in the many conversations with the institutional partner over the past four years, he noticed that when the institutional partner was particularly interested in getting something, his voice rose very slightly. A minute into the conversation, Pete realized that his voice was up slightly, hence his note to not budge on the price.

ENTERPRISE RISK MANAGEMENT

Your field of interest will have its ups and downs, which will test your young company, sometimes in ways you would never imagine. It will take all your Keys to Success and Pearls of Wisdom to survive.

Anticipating risk and doing risk analysis based on exogenous factors is important to ease decision-making when those ugly factors arrive.

Entering 1990, the real estate world was on fire, but the seeds of its demise had already been planted. Savings and Loans and banks had decided that they, too, could make big bucks in commercial real estate. The result was that in 1991 the wheels came off all the carts at the same time.

Most commercial real estate markets were significantly overbuilt with vacancies in the low 20 percent range. Owners of real estate had no pricing power to attract tenants. Some office building owners in Denver decided it was better to not lease as the cost of procuring a tenant was more than the rent they would receive over the lease term. That is how bad it was.

In the financial world, the federal government was forced to impose drastic limitations on the ability of banks and savings and loans to provide real estate financing. Many financial institutions went under. Others were taken over by the government with a new set of specialized regulations. Risk-adverse bankers faced possible criminal and financial liability for their behavior.

The McGill world began to fall apart. No amount of anticipatory risk management would have helped. The financial partner for Columbia Business Center went out of business and was taken over by a West Coast developer, who forced us out. At Columbia Corporate Park, our financial partner, Merritt, was unable to meet the cash requirements of the bank that was financing the project. The only project without any partners, Bel Air Town Center, had been financed by Crossland, one of the savings and loans now managed by a government entity, the Resolution Trust Corporation. The loan had come due. There was no financing available to pay off Crossland.

Company cash flow was drying up quickly. Lawyers were saying that bankruptcy, both personal and otherwise, was inevitable. There seemed to be no way out, and no vision of what was to come. Things got worse as Pete's marriage was breaking up. All McGill Development employees were laid off and the two of us were left to salvage whatever we could.

It was an emotional time. Everything that we had worked for was evaporating in front of us. Worst of all, walking away was not an option. There were personal guarantees to the banks, made when it seemed the guarantees would never be called. While the banks held this power over us, they were powerless to do anything for fear of violating new rules promulgated by the regulators. Demand for payment letters from the banks would arrive, and we would write back saying the letters had arrived, and we would continue to pursue the completion and leasing of our projects. Being an entrepreneur looked like a very bad choice.

Then a sliver of a ray of sunshine—a **Pearl of Wisdom!**

Amid the chaos, there was a developer in Philadelphia, Bill Rouse, who was going through the same hell. Notes were compared and this is what Bill had to say over the phone.

PEARL OF WISDOM:
"Someday this will all be over. No one will remember how much money was lost or how many properties were given back to the lenders. The only things people will remember is how you conducted yourself and whether you filed for personal bankruptcy."

Bill went on to say that all his advisors had told him personal bankruptcy was inevitable. He responded that he would never, ever file for personal bankruptcy regardless of the situation. He also refused to get down in the gutter with the banks despite their despicable treatment of him. He was living for another day and positioning himself as best he could to be back in the game.

PEARL OF WISDOM:
This was a supreme WHY NOT ME moment and a huge Pearl

of Wisdom—stick to your principles and be who you are, even in the very worst of times. Bill's advice was followed. No bankruptcy and stay out of the gutter with the banks, regardless of their behavior.

WHY NOT ME was necessary both in the business and on a personal level. On the business side, we became non-confrontational with the banks and burnished our reputation for being straightforward and honest.

The bank on the Columbia Corporate Park (AT&T) deal offered to release all our personal liability on their loans if McGill's interest in the project was transferred to our partner, Leroy Merritt. This would enable the bank to do a separate workout with Merritt.

Despite being told on the phone by the bank that this offer was good only if agreed to immediately on the call, we checked with Leroy. Was this good for him?

He responded that he was going under if we did not do this. We agreed on the spot to do it. The bank was satisfied.

The Crossland Savings Bank loan on Bel Air Town Center had come due. Capital markets were completely shut down, and no lender could be found to refinance the shopping center. By then the savings bank had been taken over by the Resolution Trust Corporation, a government corporation for failed banks. Channeling Bill Rouse, we continued our efforts to look for financing, reported our failures to the RTC, and behaved like gentlemen.

At some point, the RTC acknowledged that refinancing was not going to happen. They were not permitted to extend the loan, except if the property was put into bankruptcy. If in bankruptcy, the

RTC could grant a five-year extension at an attractive rate. Our response was that, while any form of bankruptcy was not desired, if the bank moved to foreclose on the shopping center, the center would file for bankruptcy. The RTC filed to foreclose, and the shopping center was put in bankruptcy.

Every bankruptcy must have a workout plan. The plan for the shopping center was a new five-year loan from the RTC with every other creditor being paid 100 cents on the dollar. The plan was approved by the RTC and the bankruptcy court. Within four years, we'd paid off all the creditors and refinanced the project. It was the only McGill property with no partners and the only one that was not lost. Food for thought.

Pete and I never filed for personal bankruptcy.

It is worth time to dwell on the fact that coming out of the 1992 recession, the only project saved was the one with no financial partners. Reflect for a moment on the Pearl of Wisdom, aha moment, on the first project that our strength was in expertise, not net worth. Reflect also on Bill Rouse's PW comments on how to behave: be yourself, be professional, and not vindictive. The lesson learned was that, at this point, expertise and experience were enough to convince the bank to stick with McGill.

PEARL OF WISDOM:
The Pearl of Wisdom here? Expertise and experience, when properly applied, are more important than capital almost every time. View capital as a transitionary necessity to control your destiny. This is not unique to real estate. Your expertise and experience are what will get you through a rotten business environment.

I do not remember giving much thought to going to work for someone else. Despite all the traumas of 1991, being an entrepreneur still seemed the best, and the most fun, way to go. It would take more than one major recession to knock some sense into my head. Fortunately, the lessons learned in 1991 did result in a more resilient business approach, significantly better enterprise risk management, and a much better ability to "feel the breeze" before it is too late.

The answer was to dive back into the mortgage banking business. Linden Associates, Inc. was created. Lender contacts from my old mortgage banking days had been maintained and new relationships at Morgan Stanley and JP Morgan provided lending sources to offer to local real estate owners.

While much of the country was still in an economic recession, there were pockets in and around Baltimore where the real estate had comfortably survived the recession. This time there was no paycheck, and it became a race to create revenue before the mortgage lender on our house came calling. We just made it.

An analysis done several years later found that real estate companies fared well if they owned two thousand or more apartment units, or if their company had a culture based in the service side of the real estate industry. My Business Model going forward became a combination of a real estate service business—mortgage banking—with, hopefully, an eventual return to real estate development. Pete and I remained good friends, but that was the end of our development business together.

RISKS YOU CANNOT CONTROL

Systemic risks and Black Swan events are, by definition, beyond the control of the business enterprise. The tendency is to ignore them, but at great peril. Not feeling a breeze when it is faint can be hazardous when the wind picks up later. The best sources of "feeling the breeze" are your senior peers in the industry. They have been around and have the perspective and scars of age. Regular consultations on these risks at national industry meetings are a given. Most often, the resulting actions take the form of expanding or reducing the volume of business in the pipeline for several years, expanding when it looks good, and husbanding resources for foul weather when it looks bad.

RISKS IN YOUR INDUSTRY

In general, every industry has a set of key variables that move up and down on different cycles. It becomes important to practice risk management at the industry level, identify these variables, and become students of their movements. Hopefully, you can anticipate their ebb and flow and ride their waves to your advantage.

Looking at these variables in real estate will give you a feeling for the variables in your field.

There are three primary areas of industry risk in commercial real estate: construction, leasing, and finance. Very rarely are these three risk areas all in good shape. Most often, one is good, one neutral, and one bad. A good strategy is to create room in your economics for a problematic construction, finance, or leasing situation. Financing risks are covered in Chapter 6 — Financing.

Solving the construction risk is generally thought to be addressed by pitting general contractors (who build the buildings) against each other when finalizing the building costs and giving the job to the low bidder. This is a waste of time, energy, and goodwill. The right time to bring the general contractor on board is at the beginning of the project, the same time as the architect and site engineer. General contractor pricing consists of their general conditions and overhead, generally about 5 percent of the total price. The other 95 percent of the price comes from the subcontractors, who work for the general contractor. By bringing the GC on board early, the developer gains his or her knowledge and expertise about substitute materials and alternative ways of construction that can save more money than through the bidding process.

The corollary in manufacturing is to bring your vendors into the process while you are designing the product. They will have many great ideas that will result in a better and less expensive product.

When you are sizing up your industry, do not hesitate to question "the way things are always done."

A good example of this is our decision on the first Arundel Mills office building over whether to build the structure with concrete or steel. Baltimore is a steel town and Washington is a concrete town. It turns out that the key variable in this decision is the level of construction activity in Washington. If Washington is slow, concrete subs will come to Baltimore and offer compelling pricing. If Washington is on fire, pricing will be unreasonably high. The first office building at Arundel Mills was concrete for the aforementioned reasons. The second building was designed for concrete, but Washington was on fire and the pricing did not work. It had to be redesigned as a steel building. My partners did not consult on this process. We could have saved time and money if they asked.

Leasing is a different animal. The desired situation is to have half of the space committed before construction starts. This rarely happens. Most tenants want to see the building under construction. One of our esteemed competitors won a competition for a large tenant by standing a long steel beam upright on his site so it appeared to be under construction. It worked and he got the tenant. The only thing to do was call and offer congratulations on a very clever strategy.

By stepping back and looking at leasing in the primary market over the past two years, it is possible to have a reasonable idea of what the demand will be and from which areas of the submarket tenants will come. From that point on, it is a matter of convincing the leasing brokerage community that the project is real, and work like mad to get into the ground and put up that first steel beam.

These two risks are manageable, but sometimes the answer is to delay the project for more favorable times. Ideally, the land contract permits this to happen. Sometimes this is not the case, the deal is lost, and the developer eats the predevelopment costs.

Does this translate into other businesses? Yes, it does. In your business, you have similar industry risks that can be managed, but not in a conventional manner. Step back and think about the risks. There may be better ways.

CHAPTER 3
LAWYERS, ACCOUNTANTS, AND CONSULTANTS: BUSINESS NECESSITIES

One of the other lessons learned from 1991 was the importance to your company of using the very best lawyers and accountants available.

This is starkly apparent in the bankruptcy world. In the bankruptcy world, not all law firms are equal. Rated A, B, and C, the A firms are the lead attorneys representing the firms that file for bankruptcy. B and C firms represent the creditors and committees established to work with the A firms to resolve bankruptcy issues. The problem arises when the company filing for bankruptcy is represented by a B or C firm. The B/C law firm is dependent on the A firms for their livelihood and is thus reluctant and intimidated when pitted against an A firm.

McGill started with a C firm, recommended by our real estate law firm. Only after receiving bad legal advice and being hammered in court, our accountant educated us on the A, B, and Cs. We switched to an A firm that changed strategies and stopped the legal bleeding.

Your business relies on legal, tax, and accounting advice in the normal course of business. It is imperative to have the requisite legal and accounting expertise on your team. As with banks, these firms often do not have the expertise you require as your business expands. Do not hesitate to upgrade these areas as you grow.

On the very first McGill deal, the legal work was awful. Calling around to find out who was the very best real estate lawyer in town, the overwhelming consensus was Neil Tabor. He was not taking new clients. Time for WHY NOT US.

I called Neil. I said we had heard of his sterling reputation and that he was not taking any new clients, but would he have lunch? Neil had a Caesar salad, and I had a banana split. He agreed to take us on and lectured me on the importance of promptly paying his bill.

Years later, I asked Neil why he took on McGill. He answered that he represented all the top real estate developers in town, and they did the same thing over and over. It was fine, but boring. Neil thought McGill might be interesting. He said his hunch was right.

THE RISKS OF SIGNING DOCUMENTS

Experience over the years with legal documents has resulted in several good practices when reviewing and, more importantly, signing documents.

PEARL OF WISDOM:
Never, ever use an electronic signature. It is not really your signature. Too easy for someone to sign your name to a document and claim you did it. Never sign signature pages that are not with the document.

PEARL OF WISDOM:
Sign in blue ink and initial every page of the document over the

print, not on a blank part of the page. Peo-
ple have been known to switch out pages.
It has happened to us several times.

PEARL OF WISDOM:
Most importantly, when you receive a document for sig-nature, print it out, find a quiet place, and slowly read the entire document before signing. Make a hard copy of what you signed and send your copy back to your lawyer.

My signature has been forged on documents. Lawyers have changed wording without noting the change in the draft and lawyers have changed pages in signed documents that altered the meaning of the text. It is much better to identify these transgressions before signing than try to rectify a situation gone bad.

As your company grows, it is a good business practice to trade up law firms, accounting firms, and other consultants. As a company's needs become more complex and sophisticated, it is appropriate to evaluate a consultant's ability to meet these needs. The firms you started with are probably not the firms for you as you grow.

A result of this experience was a strong preference at Linden Associates, Inc. to hire consultants and third-party contractors rather than go in-house with full-time employees.

FOOL ME ONCE, SHAME ON YOU.
FOOL ME TWICE, SHAME ON ME.

Around 2006, Linden, feeling the faint breeze, pulled in its horns and managed to avoid the impact of the Great Recession of 2008. The analytic metric most important to the growth of our business was the annual increase in white-collar employment. Simply put, if this number is not growing, the demand for office space is not growing. In 2006 this metric was zero. There was no growth in office employment, hence no growth in office demand.

Having been humbled in the early 1990s, Linden Associates was a much more conservative operation. Being laid off at Rouse was bad enough, but laying off the workforce at McGill was even worse. These people had trusted us, bought into the vision, and dedicated several years of their lives to the endeavor. They were friends. But they were not blind to what was happening in and around the firm. When the axe fell, most marveled that we had lasted so long. Advising that real estate was probably not the best choice at the time, every employee quickly found a job with greater pay than they were making at McGill.

CHAPTER 4
MARKETING

What Are You Really Selling?

Ask a businessperson what they sell, and they usually answer with their product. But that is not at all what they are *really* selling. They are selling an experience, and the opportunity to associate and identify with a specific brand. If the business is good at this, they are the *only* company selling that experience and their product.

In the introductory marketing course I took in graduate school, the professor highlighted the "Four Ps"—Product, Price, Promotion, and Place. Marketing is not just advertising. It encompasses how you make your product, what you charge for it, how you tell the market about it, and how you bring it to market. Each of these Ps is important in building a resilient, profitable company.

Product is more than just making it. How will it be used? What color or colors should it come in? How should it be packaged? For example, take a mundane item: earbuds. Fifty years ago—if they even existed—they were hardly used. Headphones were the only item of choice for listening, but they were big, mussed up your hair, and probably had to cover your entire ear to amplify the sound. They plugged into large machines that generated the sound.

At some point, technology advanced, and the sound amplification could fit into a smaller device. Cords improved so that sound could travel a short distance from the machine to the ear. The transistor radio changed the market for earphones. Now there was a handheld device that needed a lightweight cord and something for around the ear. Some very bright person came up with the idea to put a bud in your ear rather than with a larger earphone that covered the ear.

Travel forward in time to the cell phone and Apple brand. The ordinary earphone became an earbud on steroids. Now there is one for each ear—left and right. Earbuds could be packaged in small plastic bags and sold on a rack for less than a dollar. But if you are Apple, you can put them in clever boxes that are puzzles to open, treat them like jewelry, and charge ten times more! Now they are also necessities for your iPhone. Want to switch to a different phone maker? Not so fast! Look at the other end of the cord where it plugs in. Apple earbuds only work on Apple products! Except in Europe, where the government is mandating more universal usage.

Thinking through product design and packaging has a big impact on price. Price is not a function of cost. It is what you think the market will pay for the experience of having the product. Margins on earbuds are pretty high, not because of cost but because of experience. Now earbuds come without wires and are a form of jewelry for those who want to look techy or want to listen to their device while skateboarding.

In 2023 as I shopped for Christmas presents, I went into the Apple store. There, next to the fancy earbuds, were the old-fashioned, over-the-head, muss-your-hair earphones! "Applefied" with different colors, sound cancellation, and prices to match. Retro!

Apple did not come up with this approach. General Motors is thought to be the first large company to take a more sophisticated look at product development. Henry Ford was the first entrepreneur to perfect the assembly line, which drove car production costs down to an affordable level. The joke of the day was that you could pick any Model T, as long as it was black. The car came only in black. General Motors rightfully thought they could compete with Ford by offering choices. They not only offered different colors, but segmented their cars by price with Cadillac, Pontiac, Buick, Oldsmobile, and Chevrolet brands. The guts of each car brand were similar, but the styling was unique to each brand. The public saw them as five different car models at five different price points. Cadillacs were much more expensive than the Chevrolets even though their production costs were similar.

Promotion has changed significantly since the arrival of social media, but the basic premise is unchanged. Put the product in—or near—the hands of someone, or something, the customer aspires to be like or would like to identify with. Betty Crocker, the fantasy gold-medal homemaker, has been identified with cake, flour, and other kitchen products for over fifty years. Her image is a stamp of approval for anything kitchen. Pro athletes inundate you with all sorts of products deemed to be manly: barbeque grills, pickup trucks, and even insurance. Social influencers are walking advertisements for anything that can be seen on their person. A 2023 example is the sudden rise in the sale of Kansas City Chiefs apparel due to the actions of a member of the opposite sex and a certain mutual attraction with a tight end on the team.

Place is a combination of putting the product where the consumer is likely to find it and moving it from the factory to the shelf. How it gets to the shelf, and where on the shelf it resides, can give the entrepreneur greater pricing power and larger gross margins. Today, this is called supply chain management.

Retailers of women's and men's clothing have made their clothing in Southeast Asia and China for many years as they are the low-cost providers. The problem is that making last-minute changes to products or responding quickly to changes in demand, whether up or down, does not work over this distance. The solution was to fly the products most susceptible to these risks from Asia to a central distribution facility in the United States, and then distribute them. This was not feasible until the development of very large cargo jets like the 747, but it shaves two to three weeks off the supply chain. This is valuable time if changes are being made for the Christmas or spring fashion seasons.

More generic retail goods can come by container. This was a standard practice until the pandemic when demand spiked, and supply chains broke. Two reasons behind this situation are not what you would think. Seaports generally have excess room at the port for containers. They charge the container owners a monthly sum to leave the container at the port. Recently, it has been cheaper for the owner to leave the container at the port than move it inland to a warehouse. Trucks also generally were limited to eight-hour days. As ports dug into how to put the supply chain back together, they realized their container storage pricing was part of the problem. They raised prices to make it more expensive to keep the container at the port and to encourage the container owner to move it quickly away from the port. Likewise, the ports worked with trucking unions to increase the hours that the port could be open.

The combination of these two changes rapidly cleared up space at the ports and expanded their capacity to move cargo off ships to inland locations. The long lines of ships that were anchored offshore quickly disappeared.

It took a crisis to figure out these impediments and make changes.

Christopher W. Kurz

In the interim, there were many possible reasons given for the supply chain breakdown, but very few of them resulted in fast improvement.

How do you create your product? What experience do you want the consumer to have in using the product? How do you get it in front of the consumer? What entices the consumer to reach out and buy it? This is all marketing.

PRODUCT DIFFERENTIATION

Probably the most significant Pearl of Wisdom business school gave me was the concept of product differentiation or having the only brand available for your customer. The concept is fairly simple. When a consumer buys a product, the seller wants the consumer to make the purchase decision on a non-monetary basis. In other words, for any reason other than a cheap price.

Apple saw their earbuds as an opportunity to further differentiate their cell phones and increase their margins.

The General Motors example is, in part, about product differentiation. Why buy a Cadillac instead of a Ford? It gave the buyer a different, better experience. Ford saw what GM did and invented the Lincoln.

There are two types of product differentiation—differentiate the Product and differentiate the Place. Both have in common the premise that it is (almost) never, ever about the money.

PEARL OF WISDOM:
If you are creating and selling a physical product, you will most often differentiate the physical aspects of

the product. However, you can also differentiate your product by how you deliver it and where the consumer can (or cannot) buy it.

If your business is about selling ideas and expertise, "Place" becomes "Approach." How you approach selling can differentiate how your customer sees your ideas, expertise, and company.

A good example of differentiation at the product level is the difference between Starbucks and Dunkin' Donuts. Both sell coffee. Starbucks has a siren logo that looks vaguely like the Statue of Liberty, opulent interiors, and a highly customized selection of drinks. At Starbucks, there is no small, medium, or large, only Tall, Grande, or Venti. Dunkin' Donuts, on the other hand, has a stylized orange runner as their logo. They do have small, medium, and large, and a straightforward selection of donuts, bagels, and other pastries. The price of the coffee is not a factor for the consumer at either store. Both companies have successfully differentiated their products on a nonmonetary basis. Consumers willingly pay more for the experiences these two companies offer.

Take a look at Starbucks and Dunkin' TV commercials. The Starbucks ads scream, "See me! I'm enjoying the Starbucks experience and sharing it with my friends." The Dunkin' ad has a famous actor serving you from the drive-in window. Both ads are great. They target the experiences that differentiate their product.

In the commercial real estate world in 1975, product differentiation was a foreign concept. The traditional mantra was "location, location, location." A superior location trumped all other considerations. The actual product, whether it be retail, office, industrial, or residential, could be generic just like everybody else's. Today, "location, location, location" has become outdated, as the necessity to go to a location to buy has vanished with the Internet and work from home.

PEARL OF WISDOM:
The location simply no longer matters as much as it used to. What does matter, and has become increasingly important, is "experience, experience, experience." Be like Starbucks and Dunkin'.

Experiences from the physical environment are everywhere. Humans have been creating them since they first used fire to warm the cave. A handicap of being passionate about real estate is that wherever one goes, there are great experiences that need to be investigated by walking off sidewalk widths, taking pictures of storefronts, or exploring how trash is removed from cool venues.

One early morning in Greenville, South Carolina, for a real estate meeting, I ventured out to take in the experience of Main Street when no one was around, and to figure out how it worked so well. I was not alone that early morning. The street was teaming with real estate colleagues doing the same thing.

Just as Starbucks has a specific experience in mind when you enter their store, today's successful commercial real estate projects have a specific experience in mind when you step on-site. As our business grew, product differentiation paired with a couple of other Pearls of Wisdom became the foundational core for the location, the design, and the "experience" of real estate projects.

PEARL OF WISDOM:
One of the foundational Pearls of Wisdom for product differen-

tiation came from a colleague, Scott Toombs. Scott's great Pearl of Wisdom was his observation that larger projects were much less risky for the entrepreneur than small ones. This Pearl of Wisdom, became known as the Toombs Rule of Real Estate—"There is no project too large."

Scott Toombs was a former Rouse Company colleague. He was a very big man, probably six foot five with a hefty build. Scott could be intimidating and knew how to be so. He was also incredibly smart and a great friend. Scott successfully developed a downtown Philadelphia retail project for Rouse, went on to work for the Canadian developer, Cadillac Fairview, and eventually went out on his own.

His first project on his own was a downtown Philadelphia skyscraper leased to a local bank. Subsequent projects became larger and larger. In a conversation with Scott, I asked, "Why only large projects?"

Scott pointed out that the development fee for our first project, a forty-thousand-square-foot building, probably did not cover our costs. On the other hand, the $4 million development fee for his $100 million deal left him with a $2 million profit after staffing the project.

Neither of us had any money. Partners were a requirement. Our partner was a local high-net-worth individual. Scott's was a major financial institution. Scott pointed out that if our project was successful, our 50 percent ownership would result in a modest cash flow. Scott's project would result in significant cash flow for him.

Christopher W. Kurz

The construction lender for our project required us and our wives to sign personal guarantees. If things went sideways, they did expect us to step in and make up the monetary shortfall. At $100 million, Scott's construction lender realized that his personal financial statement was inconsequential. He would not be asked to guarantee the construction loan. What the bank wanted was for Scott to be around to use his expertise to finish the project—a completion guarantee.

Scott summed it up by saying, "Why would you waste time on a small project with greater personal risk when you can do much larger projects with less personal financial risk and a much higher upside?"

Scott was absolutely right.

This Pearl of Wisdom would shape the direction of McGill Development and Linden Associates.

While Scott did these megaprojects, Baltimore did not have the market demand to support them. In the Baltimore market at the time, an office building of 75,000 to 100,000 square feet was right-sized. The comparable retail footprint was 15,000 to 40,000 square feet. To build larger was to court disaster.

The Baltimore solution was to do mixed-use projects. One of the benefits of buying a larger parcel of land is that the parcel can accommodate a variety of uses while leaving enough land for what the developer intends to build and own.

That is what we did—bought larger parcels and sold off land for the development of compatible uses by others. Retail, hotel, daycare, and residential are all compatible uses. Selling parcels for these uses also helps retire land costs at a faster pace. There is synergy when these uses are combined. The overall parcel becomes "mixed-use." Bingo! Your parcel is now seen differently than other single-use parcels. Product differentiation to the extreme! As amenities have become more popular in real estate projects, the amenity value of these other uses has increasingly benefited the developer's parcels both in marketing and in her pocketbook.

The Baltimore solution was to put multiple buildings on a large site, phased so that while there might ultimately be 300,000 square feet of office on the site, it would be phased in 100,000 square-foot segments based on demand. This made feasible the application of Scott's rule to the Baltimore market and formed our business model—large, mixed-use projects in metropolitan Baltimore. This model proved to be very successful. Until it wasn't.

If product differentiation can work for coffee, cars, earbuds, and real estate, it will work for you.

Sometimes product differentiation works as intended, and sometimes it works in unintended ways.

INTENDED: GOOD DESIGN

Quality pays for itself. There is a noticeable difference between good design and great design. When Apple came out with the iPhone, the packaging and phone design were a big step above the competition. The design clearly differentiated their product from the competition, and buyers happily paid a premium. When Tesla came to market with their first electric car, its design separated them from the competition. Their buying process (think Place) was also unique—no dealerships. Both companies coupled great design with premium quality, which instilled admirable consumer loyalty.

Great design and top quality must go together. For example, online retailers, with great designs and mediocre quality, are drowning in returns of inferior merchandise, which is one of the reasons that brick-and-mortar retail has remained the preferred mode of shopping for quality merchandise. You can verify the quality at the store and pass on clothing missing stitching or not fitting correctly.

In commercial real estate, great design backed up by excellent quality makes a huge difference. Start with curb appeal. Great design just looks better. More thought goes into the user experience inside and outside the building. Would you want your customers to come to a mediocre office building when they could come to a realy nice building? It speaks volumes about how your company views a commitment to quality and the customer.

UNINTENDED: PARKING LOT LIGHTS

Sometimes product differentiation works in ways never imagined. It has long been our practice to circle back after winning or losing a business deal to find out what happened, and why. It is amazing what you learn. A relatively large company decided to lease space at the Arundel Mills project. After they had signed the lease, we took the broker who brokered the deal to lunch.

Midway through lunch, the broker was asked, "So, why did your client decide to come to Arundel Mills?"

His response was that I would never guess what had moved the deal our way. Location? No. Sustainability (always hoping that was a reason)? No. Cheap rent (always hoping that was never the reason)? No. After several more unsuccessful guesses, he sat back and, with an air of satisfaction, said, "The lights in your parking lot."

What? Why? His client is a multinational corporation. Their employees are in the office at all hours, working with customers around the globe. Office parking lot safety in the middle of the night was a big concern.

The broker wanted to know how we were so smart to have large, shopping center-styled lights in the parking lot instead of the small, semi-decorative lights normally used.

The answer was that we were not really that smart. I had learned about parking lot lighting at The Rouse Company, where all the lights were for shopping centers. It was all I knew. We'd spent no more than fifteen minutes on the lights while building the project. Product differentiation was not intentionally at work here.

PEARL OF WISDOM:
But in the marketplace, it definitely was. The Pearl of Wisdom, other than to use big shopping center lighting in office parks? It is a good practice to take the time to follow up after the sale, win or lose, to find out what the customer's decision process was. You will be surprised more than you think.

PRODUCT DIFFERENTIATION— DIFFERENTIATING THE APPROACH

As powerful as differentiating the product is, differentiating the approach can be equally powerful. Differentiating the approach is like tilting the playing field to your advantage. Much of marketing is providing a solution to a problem the customer has. Your challenge is finding out what the problem is so you can propose a solution, hopefully, one that involves using your product. It is like learning how to ask the same question differently to elicit a response that tells you more clearly what the customer's problem is. Often, the customer is having a hard time herself articulating the problem. Your ability to help clarify the problem becomes part of the solution and makes you the one to solve the problem.

A key WHY NOT ME moment was the realization that, more often than not, pivoting your approach to a transaction can make you the only viable candidate to make the deal. The following stories feature a pivot on the approach, which made the positive difference.

THE JOINT ECONOMIC COMMITTEE

Needing a place to live during my senior year resulted in a job as a dorm counselor in the freshman dorms. One of the other dorm counselors had spent the prior summer as an intern for the Joint Economic Committee on Capitol Hill in Washington DC. That sounded like a lot of fun, and he was willing to provide an introduction on the Republican side of the staff to the Joint Economic Committee. I made contacts and wrote letters to the staff contacts my friend gave me. In the spring, I received a letter saying there would be no interns that summer.

WHY NOT ME kicked in. Time to pivot. During spring break, my visit to the Committee indicated that the Republicans were not aware that the Democrats had sent out this "no interns" letter. It was now a partisan matter. A decision was made to have Democratic and Republican interns, and luckily, the most senior Republican member of Congress on the Committee decided that the only reason they had this internship was because of the persistence of this kid from Wharton. If he wanted the job, it was his. I spent that summer on Capitol Hill, working for the Joint Economic Committee.

In August the committee had hearings on manufactured housing. This was not a high priority amongst the staff, so this intern got the opportunity to do most of the legwork. It proved to be very interesting and was the first indication that I had a passion lurking inside for real estate. This passion grew.

One of the benefits of the Congressional Intern Program was a robust educational and social program of lectures, sessions with congressmen, embassy parties, and parties elsewhere throughout Washington. In early June, there was a party at a nice house on the Potomac River. Upon entering the living room, I saw this incredible woman sitting on the edge of the couch. The only thing I remembered from that evening was that she went to Mount Holyoke College and worked for a senator from Alaska. There were only two senators from Alaska, so the odds were 50-50 of finding the right office. WHY NOT ME time.

Late Monday morning, I tried the first senator's office. Did they have an intern from Mount Holyoke College? Yes, they did. What was her name? Debbie King. Is she here?

Lunch later that week was followed by a series of dates. That fall, Debbie was living with her parents in Washington and going to Georgetown University. She visited Penn several times, and by early the following year, we were engaged. Wow. Still married after all these years.

AT&T

Occasionally, Pete and I would carpool together from Baltimore to the office in Columbia, Maryland, for an opportunity to talk with no one around. We would always drive by an eighty-eight-acre site owned by AT&T, which originally had been bought for a manufacturing facility that was never built. One evening, one of us observed that at some point, some smart developer would make a deal with AT&T to buy the site. It would not be us, and we would be pissed. Truly a WHY NOT US moment was on the table. We put in a lot of thought on how to approach AT&T and how to craft an attractive deal that met their needs.

Pete had a second cousin who knew one of the top people at AT&T. We went in at the senior level and were passed down to the head of real estate. It never hurts to go in at the top. AT&T had no plans to sell the property, but they might give it some consideration. We accepted an invitation to meet with AT&T in Basking Ridge.

PEARL OF WISDOM:
We drove up in Pete's Mercedes convertible. Never underestimate the power of a fancy sports car. It sends an unambiguous message of success.

One of the challenges with AT&T was to prove that the McGill Development Company had the expertise and chops to build an eighty-eight-acre project. We brought a nationally recognized architectural and engineering firm on board to do the initial design. A well-known insurance company agreed to write a letter expressing interest in financing the project without making any firm commitments.

AT&T eventually decided they were interested in joint venturing the site. It was time to bring Product Differentiation into the mix, not in the design of the project, but in the crafting of a proposal that would be completely different from the competition's. The gist of the proposal was that AT&T is a very large company and McGill is a very small company. McGill could not hope to understand all the specific needs AT&T would have in this venture. But we could say to AT&T that if they shared what was important to them, McGill would be completely transparent and try our best to meet those needs. This message was hammered home consistently and, eventually AT&T tried us out on a few small items. This led to bigger items. As a result, McGill was awarded the project in the form of a highly complicated joint venture.

As AT&T worked its way through its approval process, the timeline slowed down. Having a very close relationship with AT&T enabled us to ask if there was a problem. There was. Senior management wanted to know why the real estate department was dedicating so much manpower to managing a complicated joint venture on a project that, in AT&T's view, was de minimis.

Would AT&T rather just sell the site?

Yes.

AT&T asked, "What do you think it's worth?"

We answered, "$12.5 million."

Their response was, "That's our number, too."

Would AT&T like a contract?

"Yes, please."

Now things got very risky for McGill. The market thought McGill had won the deal as a very complicated joint venture. They had stopped paying attention. If anyone learned that it was now simply the acquisition of a site, all the competitors would jump back in, raise the price, and most likely move McGill out of the picture.

Pete and I didn't usually have lunch together, but if something came up, lunch was code for time to leave the office for a private conversation. We had lunch that afternoon. One of us drove to our lawyer's office in Baltimore, brought him up to date, and asked him to draft a contract. When the contract was ready, I drove back to his office to sign the contract, and he sent it off to AT&T. Aside from the two of us and our lawyer, no one else in the office, or, we hoped, the world, had any inkling of what was happening. Two weeks later, the contract was signed by AT&T.

Some thought had been given to potential financial partners. The following Monday was George Washington's birthday. It was time to get on the phone and hunt for money. The first two calls went to voicemail, but the third was answered by a large industrial developer, Leroy Merritt. Leroy was brought up to date on the phone and his response was "What are you doing now?"

I answered, "Talking to you while my seven-year-old son, Tim, is coloring on my office floor."

Leroy said, "Come on over. Let's talk."

Tim and I went to see Leroy. We talked about the project for about half an hour. Leroy asked what type of deal we wanted: a 50-50 joint venture with him providing the necessary financial strength to go to the bank. Leroy stood up, reached out his hand, and said he would do that deal. We shook hands, and Leroy turned to Tim. "Let's go get a coke." That was it.

PEARL OF WISDOM:
The Pearl of Wisdom from the story is never take off George Washington's birthday.

THE HORSE FARM

This story is about listening and differentiating your product. It is also about managing your supply chain, knowing the chain, and listening to what your vendors tell you. They know your business and are often a great source of business intelligence.

Previously, I mentioned the importance of the Urban Land Institute. One morning, as I walked out of an executive meeting of the Baltimore Chapter with the chair, I asked what he was up to. Among other things, he mentioned that his firm had been retained by the University of Maryland to sell several agricultural properties. Until then, if the university sold a real estate asset, the proceeds went to the general fund for the state. The policy was changed so that the funds would go to the department that owned the property, in this case, the Agricultural School. He mentioned that one of the properties was at a prime intersection immediately north of Columbia, Maryland, twenty acres in size (WHY NOT ME!!!!). He agreed that when the request for proposals (an RFP) to purchase the site was released, my new development company, Linden Associates, Inc., would be included.

The RFP arrived and was reviewed by us. It required the submission of a proposed site plan and a purchase price for the twenty acres. The site had been part of a much larger parcel which was now divided by a new outer Beltway, Route 100, that ran around southwestern Baltimore. The site would have to be rezoned given the smaller size.

By this time, I was well-known in Columbia, and Howard County where Columbia is located. Having built three projects totaling almost 500,000 square feet in the county, we had an excellent relationship with the Planning Department. Given the unique location of the site and the rezoning requirement, it made sense to reach out to the Department Head of Planning and Zoning for his opinions on what this site was best suited for. The department head was a very reserved and proper individual. After the normal salutations on the phone call, he immediately got to the point about the horse farm.

He said: "I know what you want to put on this property and there is no ******* way this is going to happen."

I responded: "Those are very strong words coming from you."

He went on: "This site is crying out to be developed as a large shopping center. It borders Route 100 and two other major highways, but that's not going to happen. The site is adjacent to Columbia, Maryland, where the grocery-anchored shopping centers are all embedded in neighborhoods. A new shopping center would decimate these smaller neighborhood retail centers. The county is not concerned with the financial impact of such a new shopping center on these existing shopping centers. But, as a matter of public policy, it would be bad for the county if a new, large shopping center caused grocery stores in these small shopping centers to close, leading to vandalism, crime, and other societal issues that the county would prefer not to deal with."

He was absolutely correct. Would he consider a Plan B—a mixed-use project with office and retail, but probably with more retail than the 20 percent allowed under the proposed zoning? I proffered that the days of office buildings floating alone in seas of asphalt are gone. Projects now must provide an experience to the user that goes beyond simply being there.

We discussed the concept for a few minutes, and he opined that he could go for something like that, but just keep the retail as small as possible.

Our plan was redone and submitted to the university along with an offer for the land. Several weeks later, offerees were invited in by the university for a presentation of their plan and to discuss their financial proposal. Each presentation was expected to last approximately one hour. The Linden meeting lasted fifteen minutes. The university asked about our proposal and why it was oriented to mixed-use (offices with some retail) instead of all retail. I mentioned the comments from the head of the planning department and his public policy concerns. The university panel asked a few other minor questions about the mixed-use nature of the plan, and that was it. I thought I had blown the opportunity.

Two weeks later, the ULI Chair called.

"Has the Head of Planning and Zoning seen the plan you presented to the university?"

"No."

"Please go see him and review your plan in detail."

The Head of Planning and Zoning was a very busy person. Usually, it takes two weeks to get a brief meeting. Upon explaining this to the ULI chair, he retorted that he would see us right away. The chair was right. He was immediately available.

We reviewed the plan in detail. He wanted higher density on the site. Normally, it is the developer who wants higher density and the public agency that says no.

He reasoned, "Since the development of Columbia started, many similar intersections have been developed at densities that ultimately turn out to be too low. Could you increase the density?"

"Absolutely."

Some specifics on the plan were nailed down and I thanked him for his time. I reported the meeting results to the ULI Chair.

A month later, the university asked for the best and final financial offer. In thinking about all that had gone on about this project, the AT&T deal came to mind. In that situation, it was intentional to differentiate our proposal on a nonmonetary basis to beat the competition. In this case, it seemed that product differentiation had happened unintentionally. Why was the first meeting so short? Why was the Head of Planning and Zoning immediately available to review the plan? It seemed like our proposal was, indeed, quite different from others. Perhaps Linden was the only qualified candidate. Maybe it was the only qualified candidate from a very small list, or maybe the university was just on a fishing expedition and there was no chance anyway.

Regardless, when the call came for the best and final offer, my answer was that the best offer had been given in the fifteen-minute meeting.

The caller did not accept this answer. "Now is the time to increase the offer to make it more competitive," he said.

The entrepreneurial part of my brain said, "Don't budge." My gut felt the same way. There was no budge. The disappointed caller hung up.

Three weeks later, the phone rang. Linden had been selected!

Six months later, the ULI chair and I were chatting, and I thanked him and the university for the opportunity to make a proposal to buy the horse farm.

"How much did you know about what was going on behind the scenes?" he asked.

"Nothing," I said.

It turned out that the university had also met with the department head before putting the property on the market. He told them the same thing he had told me. When the proposals came in, every other proposal was for the large shopping center.

When quizzed about the ability to rezone the property, the developers assured the university they had the contacts to make it happen.

The one question the university wanted to ask me in the interview was, "Why did you talk to the head?" They went back to the department head and asked if any other developers had asked him about the site.

"Nobody else asked," he responded. "If they had, I would have told them the same thing."

Why did we talk to the head? The project had to pass muster with his department, hence he was like a vendor. His input made for a better product, *and* it got us the deal!

So, unintentionally, product differentiation was alive and well. The ULI chair also said they had set a minimum price below which the property would not be sold. The Linden offer was comfortably above that price, but much lower than all the other offers. Ultimately, the university decided that the likelihood of a successful rezoning with the Linden site plan was worth the lower price.

Christopher W. Kurz

Normally, when rezoning a property, one hires a land-use attorney to present the case. In Howard County at that time, the two best land attorneys were representing clients with controversial cases.

When the head asked who our attorney was going to be, I answered, "None of the above."

There was a pause, and then the head said, "That will be just fine." The reality was that the size of the parcel was the only thing that required a zoning change in the proposed use of this site.

It also helped a lot that, while working for Rouse, we had lived in the neighborhood where the project was located.

At the meeting with the neighborhood association, we all rem-inisced about the farms that were no longer there, and Toddler Time, a preschool that my wife had started. Several members of the board had put their kids in Toddler Time. I was no longer the evil outsider, but the returning neighbor. The chair wanted to know why I, the company president, would come to the neighbor-hood meeting. Wasn't it normal to send the planner and lawyer to avoid having to answer tough questions? My response was that they were entitled to quiz me and check me out.

"Where are your plans?" they said, expecting detailed drawings.

My response was, "Until there is community input, the plans could not be finalized."

When the zoning hearing was held the neighborhood association got up to speak.

They said, "The developer does not know that the association planned to come to the zoning hearing and does not know what the association is going to say."

They said to the zoning board that they have met with me and think Linden Associates is the best firm to develop this property. The association fully supported the rezoning request.

Silence. The zoning board quickly approved the project and the process moved on to the County Council, where it was also approved.

Linden Associates ultimately partnered with Merritt and developed the horse farm. A major reason for partnering with Merritt, aside from our history, was their willingness to take all of the financial risks of the project. Since the AT&T days, Merritt had become partners with a large institutional partner at the corporate level. This partner had demonstrated a willingness to back every project that Merritt had undertaken since AT&T. Even though it meant giving up leadership and control of the development to Merritt, as a humbler developer, I was happy to make the deal.

SOWING THE SEEDS

As your business grows, certain phrases and attitudes become unique to your company. They also serve to differentiate you from the competition at the beginning of a business relationship. No one else does what you do, or sees the world the way you do. Three of these unique thoughts about real estate design evolved: The double-wide, the two-scoop ice cream cone, and the *Sunday*

New York Times. These are all a part of product differentiation at the product level and at the presentation and negotiation level.

Sidewalks have been eight feet wide since roads had cars. As walking became more prevalent, the eight-foot sidewalk became functionally obsolete. How wide does a sidewalk have to be, not only to function, but to provide a comfortable experience? The answer is: Wide enough so that two fathers (or mothers), each pushing a double-wide baby stroller with twins on board, can comfortably pass on the sidewalk. This is a minimum of twelve feet. Sixteen is better.

Today, outside dining has become very popular. Sidewalks should be wide enough for the double-wide's, plus two rows of tables. My competition pays no attention to sidewalk widths. Espousing a sixteen-foot-wide sideway gets people thinking. The double-wide story resonates with everyone and is hard to forget.

You have probably bought your family ice cream cones and eaten them in the car. There is nothing special about this. How many times have you bought two-scoop ice cream cones, especially for the kids, and eaten them in the car? Probably never more than once. The best place to eat a two-scoop ice cream cone is on a bench or at a table close to the ice cream store with lots of napkins. The design requirements to create a public space conducive to a family eating two-scoop ice cream cones sets the space apart (product differentiation) in a very positive way from most other public space designs. Like the double-wide's, this story brings a unique flair to a discussion on park amenities. It is also hard to forget.

Reading the *Sunday New York Times* is best done in a leisurely manner in a serene, pleasant environment. Most people have had this experience and can relate to the desired setting. Putting the setting outside in a public area, the listener immediately contrasts their experience with known public areas, none of which are conducive to reading the *Sunday Times*. What would a public space have to be like for you to want to take the newspaper and a cup of coffee (Starbucks, Dunkin', or your local brand) outside to read? It would have to be pretty special. The *Sunday New York Times* test is a verbal description of the quality of the public areas intended for the development. Also, it is hard to forget.

All three of these mantras—sidewalk width, double ice cream cones, and park environment—serve to improve the quality of the project beyond what is envisioned and to separate Linden from the competition at the site acquisition and public approval point.

CHAPTER 5
DEMOGRAPHICS, STATISTICAL ANALYSIS, AND YOUR GUT

Your Indispensable Crystal Balls

They did not teach demographics in business school, but they should have. They did teach statistics, but statistics today, thanks to increases in computing power, is used in ways never before imagined. Think of baseball and football.

DEMOGRAPHICS

A key part of any successful business is the owner's ability to see into the future and discern their best direction from the information at hand. What if you had the ability to see into the future? To see around the corner before turning? Demographics and the analysis of industry data can give you that ability.

Every ten years, the U.S. Government conducts a nationwide census of the population. The census is much more than a tally of how many of us there are. It includes information on families, education levels, income levels, and ethnic backgrounds. All are parsed down to census tracts that are smaller than most political jurisdictions.

It is interesting to look at the changes in this data from census to census. These changes tell you about trends. Applying these trends to your business can tell you what is happening in your market. Extending these trends forward will give you clues as to what will happen in your market. The downside is that the census is only every ten years. However, this is not a problem. The demographic data that the census gathers is also available on an annual basis in most political jurisdictions. Your industry also produces data that can be used along with demographic data to bridge the ten-year gap.

McGill did just this at the Bel Air shopping center. The most recent census data was nine years old and did not reflect the explosive population growth in Bel Air. Most retailers use census data to gauge market strength. Knowing that the old census data would not be accurate, or support retailers entering the Bel Air market, we built our own database using county data on housing starts, prices, education levels, and school population growth to more accurately reflect the current market. If we could get the retailer to accept our analysis, we usually signed a lease.

Today, data from cell phones can tell you not just how many people are in a given location at a specific time, but you can determine which stores they are going to. The metric used to be how many cars went by a location in a twenty-four-hour period. Thanks to technology, this metric is now not nearly as important as cell phone data. If you are a retailer, statistical analysis now tells you what other stores your customers shop at, and how frequently. A location next to these shops now becomes very attractive. A good leasing agent already will have done the cell phone data analysis and will show his retailer client exactly where to locate.

In the 1990s, there was a large population movement by young adults into cities across the country. Census data quantified this movement. The question is, was it a permanent change in housing preferences? All the data suggested this was so. However, in the appendix of one such study, young adults were asked about their

Christopher W. Kurz

aspirational housing choices. The appendix showed that young adults aspired to the traditional suburban single-family house with the white picket fence, but not until they were married and starting a family. They also wanted the amenity level they were enjoying in the city to follow them to the suburbs.

So, data by itself is interesting, but read the appendix and seek out professionals who can help you interpret the data.

This has played out across the country, as close-in suburbs have been the big beneficiaries. Have the popular areas of the cities suffered? No. The parents of these young people visited their off-spring in the cities, liked the atmosphere, and moved in. If you are a city retailer, the market is still there, but the customer has changed. The popular bars probably empty out sooner on Saturday nights.

If your market is the new home buyer, it is important to know where young adults are moving when they leave the city. They do not generally move to the nearby suburbs. In Baltimore people living southeast of Baltimore City tend to leapfrog across the city to the northwest suburbs. Why? Baltimore is thirty-five miles north of Washington, D.C. Washington area housing is about 30 percent more expensive than Baltimore. The Washington economic influence makes housing south and west of Baltimore too expensive. The suburbs with an economic profile similar to southeast Baltimore are northwest of the City.

If you are a Baltimore Realtor, it is smart to have offices in southeast Baltimore as well as the northwest. If you sell furniture, appliances, banking services, or home improvements, you also will benefit from having both offices. But do not expect the southeast office to have high sales volumes. That office brings the customer to the office in northwest Baltimore. Likewise, if you have a restaurant in southeast Baltimore and want to expand, go where your existing customers are moving to, not just down the road.

Every two years, we would ask the brokerage firm, CBRE, to do a statistical analysis of the metropolitan office market, including changes in supply and demand by submarket. The reason for this data exercise is that, even though we are local and think we know the submarkets, things do change in markets you are not currently active in. Submarkets that were thought strong two years ago turned out to be not so strong, and ones that were weak now look much more interesting. Not relying on just the numbers, we followed up with a lengthy meeting with the CBRE brokers to discuss the data, ask for their interpretation, and ask for their crystal-ball look at which submarkets might have long-term potential and why. This led us to some unanticipated projects that were very profitable and away from some areas that our competitors dove into with poor results.

STATISTICAL ANALYSIS

The increase in computing power and the use of statistical analysis has changed nearly every business, but the change is easily seen in professional baseball and football. If your team does not use the latest analytical tools, you will lose no matter how talented your players and coaches are.

The Oakland A's were probably the first baseball team to use modern analytics to determine exactly which metrics and talents actually made a difference in team performance. Michael Lewis wrote *Money Ball* to show how successful these tools could be. Today, the combination of video and analysis allows a team to parse a player's ability and tendencies and make adjustments that vastly improve their performance. Teams now have departments that do this work, and they drive the organization.

In baseball, teams now know where a batter is most likely to hit the ball given the count (balls and strikes), inning, score, and pitcher. The results were defensive alignments that dared the batter to hit the ball to areas with no fielders. Amazingly, the batters rarely were able to do so! Recently, these alignments have been outlawed to limit the use of these metrics to benefit the defense.

In the "old" days, the catcher gave the pitch sign to the pitcher using his fingers between his legs, where only the pitcher could see them. Today, it is too easy to intercept the signs using miniature cameras hidden in the outfield. Now the catcher has a pad on his shin guard and the signal is sent electronically to a receiver in the pitcher's hat. Harder to steal, unless you know the radio frequency.

In pro football (and probably in top college programs), every play of your opponent is sliced and diced to identify it seconds before the ball is hiked. Coaches no longer have to look at the opponent's formation to figure out the next play. They can read key defensive player movements as soon as the play starts to know how to change their play after the ball is hiked.

The impact can best be described by recounting a play during a recent Super Bowl. Close to the goal line, the offense knew that the defense used their analytic prowess to understand each and every tendency of their offense. They needed a play that looked like one they ran frequently, but was different. All they needed to do was get the all-pro cornerback to make a quick read, identify the play as one frequently used, and make one step to his left. That step would free their end to fake to his right and go left across the goal line. They had created that play the week before, anticipating just this moment. They ran the play. The all-pro stepped to his left. The end faked right, ran left, and caught a touchdown pass.

In business, similar analytics and consumer-behavior research is used to identify competitor weaknesses. Small changes in your product line as a result of these analytics can significantly differentiate your product, improve your market share, and increase profitability.

YOUR GUT

In the first *Star Wars* movie, Luke Skywalker trains to become a Jedi master with Yoda. Yoda keeps saying, "Feel the power of the Force." Eventually, Luke gets the message and learns to trust the power of the Force and use it to his advantage. While I cannot (yet) move a pencil into my hand using the Force, I have learned the real-life equivalent—feel the power of your gut. More often than not, while the statistics and demographics say one thing, your gut tells you to do something different.

You should not only listen to your gut, but the guts of trusted people close to you. They have the benefit of not being as near to a situation as you are and seeing things differently. Phrases like, "This may be better than you think," or "I would not do that if I were you," should set off alarm bells in your mind.

Listen to the collective wisdom of the guts.

Numerous times in a business situation when you confront a supposedly stronger force, the first reaction is to cover and run. But your gut says no. To borrow from basketball, sometimes the best strategy is to drive to the basket, into your bigger opponent, and confront their strength. Such bigger opponents are often not at ease dealing with the smaller, quicker player they normally intimidate. It does not always work, but it often does. Try it.

CHAPTER 6
FINANCE

The Unfortunate Necessity of Other People's Money

Money is an unfortunate necessity in starting a business. Money comes from lending institutions, equity partners, or your own pockets. The goal of any successful entrepreneur is to wean oneself off the first two options. In the interim, there is no choice but to live with them.

There are two components of risk in the financial marketplace: liquidity and credit. Liquidity is a measure of how easy it is to quickly sell something you own. In the business world, what you own is known as an "asset." Credit is a measure of how likely it is one can raise money. If it is your credit that is being evaluated, it is how likely you will be able to find money. If you are providing the money, the credit of the other party is the likelihood that you will get your money back. Good credit is lending to the U.S. government. Bad credit is lending money to your no-good cousin.

Typical assets are a stock, a bond, your house, your million-square-foot real estate project, your yacht, your savings account at the bank, or your loan to your cousin. You pay a price to buy the asset and receive a return. With a savings account, you put the money in the bank, and the bank pays you interest. That is your "return." The annual return from the stock, bond, or savings account is also called the "yield." If you put $100 in a savings account at the bank, and it pays a 5 percent interest rate, your balance at the end of the year would be $105. Your annual return, or yield, is 5.0 percent. You can take your money out of the bank anytime you want. It is "liquid." Think of water. It is literally and figuratively a liquid. You can pour it into a glass, on a plant, or into the bathtub. Now freeze the water. As ice, it has limitations on its use. Maybe as ice cubes, but not for the plant and, unless you really want to, not in the bathtub. It is no longer liquid. It is "illiquid."

Unlike stocks, bonds, or savings accounts, real estate (and the loan to the cousin) is not liquid. If you are dissatisfied with your stock or bond, or you want your money back, a quick phone call, the investment is sold, and you have your money back. Not so easy with real estate (or the cousin). It is illiquid.

A vital component of any investment is where it stands in the line of creditworthy alternatives. How risky is the investment?

Picture a bank teller's window with a long line of creditors wanting to borrow money. Their place in line is based on their creditworthiness. The first person in line is Uncle Sam. U.S. government debt is considered the least risky investment asset one can have. Behind Uncle Sam are municipalities and large corporations with high credit ratings. They must pay a slightly higher yield than Uncle Sam to entice investors to buy their stocks and bonds. About three-quarters of the way through the line, behind the companies with good but lesser credit ratings, is commercial real estate. It can be argued that commercial real estate should be farther up the queue, but the reality is that, due to the illiquid nature of the investment and the complicated aspects of the investment, which most people do not understand, its spot

Christopher W. Kurz

three-quarters of the way back is merited. Your cousin is at the end of the line.

There is no assurance that when your turn at the window comes, there will be money available to borrow. At the beginning of a recession, the "bank window" is open only to those with the highest credit. During good times, it is open to just about anyone.

BANKING

The following comments about banking and dealing with banks are very biased. Having worked for a bank, having founded a bank, and having borrowed millions of dollars from banks, these are personal opinions, perhaps right, perhaps wrong, about the necessary evil of doing business with financial institutions.

All banks are not the same. They like doing business with certain types of people and very reluctantly do business with other types. The banking expertise your company needs probably does not reside in the part of the bank you have exposure to. For example, if you are in retail, cash management and credit card services are important banking services. This expertise does not reside at the local branch, but the manager will be game to try before passing you on to the right people.

As a real estate company, collecting and depositing rent is a significant banking need. Initially, the rent checks would come to the office, and someone would go to the bank every day to deposit the checks. Banks would offer a service to have the checks come to them and be deposited, but this service is expensive. Our accountant introduced us to the Annapolis, Maryland, office of Merrill Lynch, which was happy to have the checks come to their office and be deposited. The deposit would show up online the next day. All for the princely sum of $300 per year. Such a deal! Why were they so much less expensive than the banks? They were not a bank! This was a normal service Merrill Lynch offered to their stock brokerage clients, no big deal. Merrill Lynch became our day-to-day bank. Still is.

Banks are risk averse. To the best of my knowledge, there has never been a bank employee who has been financially or otherwise rewarded for taking a risk for a customer. People who are not risk averse generally do not last working at banks.

Commercial banks, as differentiated from investment banks and private equity, make their money by doing the same things over and over again in a very disciplined manner. Car loans, mortgages, checking accounts, and certificates of deposit are all fairly straightforward. Banks make their money over the life of an asset, primarily as interest and fees. With the checks and balances that most banks have, this is a great recipe for making money a nickel at a time. It may be boring, but it works. When banks decide that this is too boring, they venture into riskier areas where they lack the expertise to succeed. The bank makes mistakes, and bad things happen.

This also works in reverse. Investment banks and private equity make their money when an asset changes hands, as in buying and selling stocks and bonds and raising capital for companies. When investment banks and private equity try to act like commercial banks, they do not have the patience or the discipline to do the boring but profitable lending that is common with regular banks. It seldom ends well.

The difference between a banker and an investment banker was explained to me by a senior investment banker. A banker and an investment banker go on a new business call. The customer is busy, says not now, and slams the door on the caller's foot.

The banker pulls his damaged foot from the doorjamb and limps home. The investment banker, in one quick move, removes the damaged foot from the doorjamb and inserts his other foot before the customer can close the door. This pretty much sums it up.

> **PEARL OF WISDOM:**
> *As an entrepreneur, your job is to find a lending institution whose culture and expertise match the nature of your business. Ask around. Who do your competitors bank with? Do they have a favorite loan officer? The best time to talk to a banker is when you do not need to do business with them. It allows you to get to know them as individuals and to learn whether or not their culture is conducive to a successful relationship with your company. As a general rule, it is good to know at least three people at your bank at all times. It is highly likely that one of those three people will leave the bank each year. If your relationship is with only one banker and that banker leaves, your relationship with the bank has just walked out the door.*

Most banks cluster their commercial loan officers at their headquarters or regional headquarters. Branch locations are designed to cater to the consumer and not the business world. To the extent that your needs go beyond the general consumer needs, a branch bank, no matter how willing, will be ill-equipped to meet your needs.

That was the premise that led to the start of the Columbia Bank in Columbia, Maryland. Six of us played tennis every Saturday morning at an indoor court. Over time, the post-playing coffee hour stretched out. Two of the participants were bankers. During one such coffee hour, one of the non-banker players commented to the bankers about the lack of commercial banking expertise at the branch level in most banks in the suburbs. What if you started a bank in the suburbs that had commercial banking expertise? The consensus was that you would make a killing. Do you sense a little product differentiation here? The next week, one of the bankers said he could not stop thinking about this possibility. Columbia, Maryland, was identified as a good location for such a bank. It took over a year to put a plan in place. Fortunately, several friends with great expertise in banking generously critiqued each version of the plan for a new bank. When it was time to raise money, no one asked a question that our mentors had not grilled us on.

The initial money raise offered a board seat in addition to the financial investment. Eventually, on a Friday evening around a swimming pool with two prospective investors, they indicated they were interested. Our response was: "We are sitting around the pool and talking about going swimming. It is time to stop talking and jump in the pool."

While they did not literally jump into the pool, they did say they were ready to go swimming. Sunday night, they called saying we were up to seven investors. They had called their friends and said they were investing in the new bank and that others should, too. The initial raise was stopped at thirty investors, meaning the bank board would have thirty people on it. Almost all those investors were successful entrepreneurs who had experienced the difficulties of banking in building their companies. They regaled us with their banking trials and tribulations.

In addition to being a different bank on the commercial banking side, The Columbia Bank was lucky enough to make an excellent hire from Household Finance to build the retail side of the bank. Mike was told not to worry about volumes, or meeting any particular goals, but just to build the bank on the retail side as he saw fit. Coming out of Household Finance, he was used to competing against banks, so he was a natural.

With these two unique banking aspects, Columbia Bank took off. The bank remained independent for years, growing beyond the billion-dollar level. It was when the other co-founder decided to retire that he found the right purchaser for the bank. A good part of the bank's long-term success was that this co-founder wanted passionately to lead a bank. The initial board members shared that passion.

In the real estate banking world, the best bank for a young, growing company is a bank that first looks at the proposed collateral, the real estate, to see if they think it passes muster. If so, the next question is, can the borrower bring this plan to fruition? And the third question is whether they are going to need financial help, a.k.a., a financial partner. Banks that are not particularly interested in financing real estate projects tend to focus first on the borrower to see if their net worth and liquidity are sufficient to repay the bank in the event of problems. During one meeting with a bank, they explained that they like to make real estate loans that are a small percentage of the borrower's net worth, not a multiple. This bank was not a match for McGill or Linden.

In the last ten years, small local banks have grown to the size where they can accommodate most real estate development lending needs. The large national banks tend to monitor their real estate lending portfolios to maintain a balance both geographically and by property type. This makes sense for the bank, but it is not very good for the local developer who finds out too late that the big bank has too much of what he or she builds.

Today, most local developers and business people develop close relationships with several local banks. They keep the banks apprised of what is in their pipeline and closely monitor each bank's lending limit concerning their business.

When Bel Air Town Center was sold, the buyer obtained a financing commitment from one of his local banks. Shortly thereafter that bank was bought by another local bank the buyer also did business with. There were several weeks of high anxiety about how the borrower's business would fit into the combined banks, both in terms of lending limits and the bank personnel to deal with the buyer. It was all resolved successfully and the deal closed, but our buyer did not anticipate that those two banks would merge.

EQUITY PARTNERS

In general, equity partners fall into four buckets: friends and family, high-net-worth individuals, short-term institutional investors, and long-term institutional investors.

The advantage of "friends and family" is that they probably know you (could be good or bad) and are relatively unsophisticated. They are buying into your philosophy and time frame. You remain in control of the venture. Their investment is in hard money with no contingent liability to a lender. If the project fails, they lose their investment and move on. While no one wants to lose money, they are more understanding of the risk and are willing to live with bad consequences. The disadvantage is that it is hard to raise large sums of equity from friends. You may shy away from exposing your business to such an intimate group, but if the desired amount of money to be raised is low, and you are professional, it is the best alternative. I have never taken this route because I did not think I knew enough people, and, in the beginning, was worried that failure would cost me my paycheck job.

This was a mistake. As life as a developer winds down, I have asked developer friends if they do "Friends and Family" capital raises. Most do, and our family now invests with these friends as a part of our overall investment strategy. It is never too late to learn.

High-net-worth individuals provide a one- or two-stop equity source. Very high-net-worth individuals probably have a family office and a disciplined approach to investing. You want these investors to have a very long-term horizon and to put up cash instead of providing bank guarantees. The best people in this category invest in your business more than the products you make. They plan to invest repeatedly as your company grows and to rely on you to pick the exit strategy. While they may have some say in major decisions, it is unlikely they will pull the plug. In this regard, their history can be checked out. These relationships generally work well.

PEARL OF WISDOM
What tends to not work so well are high-net-worth individuals whose own financial strength is new and dependent on the success of their business. Their patience with you may be influenced by their own travails. You should avoid these investors who want to put up bank guarantees instead of cash investments. If things go south, they will move to protect their interest and hang you out to dry.

Most institutional investors—life companies, Real Estate Investment Trusts, pension funds, and investment banker-sponsored funds—say they are long-term. But they are not. They are driven by financial returns, and once the returns level out, they want out.

Their deals give them the right to force a sale. If you are happy with a five to seven-year time frame this may be the deal for you. If not, plan to take out your institutional partner within this time frame, and make sure your investment documents give you that right within a comfortable amount of time.

Most likely, your passion is not real estate, but read on and see the similarities and differences between our passions.

One investment vehicle to keep in mind is the "Texas Put." In simple terms, it says that, at any point in time, one partner may buy out the other. The initiating partner names the price and the amount each partner will receive. The other partner chooses to buy or sell at that price. The put, when initially documented, lays out the timeline for how long the receiving partner has to choose to buy or sell, and how long the deal has to close. This might seem simple, and you might think the advantage goes to the wealthier partner, but this is not so. The not so wealthy partner has time to put their deal together before implementing the put. We almost did this once with an institutional partner. It was not necessarily due to Pete's listening ability, but the Put was always in the background.

We did do a Texas Put on another project. The existing financing was coming due, and our mortgage banker said a refinance would give us the cash to buy the property if the other party chose to sell. It took a long time, and it was hard to pick the strike price where we were willing to be either the buyer or the seller. We figured out a workable strike price and instigated the Texas Put. Ultimately, the other party bought us out.

YOUR OWN POCKETS

The best option of all is if you have the funds. If you do not have the funds today, the key here is to look down the road—five to seven years—and see if there might be a strategy that enables the buyout of an existing partner. It may entail a new partner on better terms. When we bought out the institutional partner at Columbia Business Center and brought in a new partner, McGill increased its ownership percentage from 10 percent to 50 percent. It might have been a great deal if the 1990 recession had not happened.

It may be the case that selling the asset is in your best interest, too. If the returns are leveling out and net sale proceeds to you can be recycled into the next deal, that next deal may be your first "no partner" deal.

The objective with these strategies is to harvest your business assets to create liquid net worth, which eventually can replace "other people's money."

CHAPTER 7
BUSINESS ANALYTICS

The KISS Principle:
Keep It Simple Stupid

Today, it is hard to imagine starting, building, and running a company without computers and the software to parse every decision. This may be "old school," but even artificial intelligence cannot make the final decision that makes or breaks your company. My first job was sitting at an IBM Selectric typewriter hooked up to a phone line connected to a computer in Washington, DC, where the software was located to do rudimentary analysis of real estate projects. Computer screens had not yet been invented.

We debated whether "net present value" or "internal rate of return" was a better feasibility measurement. Remembering back to the finance chapter and our 5 percent return on our savings account, these two measurements incorporate the lifetime of the investment to calculate your "yield" over the holding period at the end when you sell or redeem your investment. This is especially relevant if the annual return goes up and down during the holding period.

PEARL OF WISDOM:
There is one correct answer to the debate about which sophis-

ticated analytical measurement tools to use.
Based on fifty years of business experience
and familarity with the tools and options,
the answer is…. none of the above!

The devil is in the details. As you move from looking at just one year of returns to multiple years, the number of variables needed for the calculations increases dramatically. Most of these variables involve guesses about changes in the future. Slight changes in each variable, while seemingly inconsequential, can significantly change the final answer.

Alex. Brown Realty Advisers represented several pension funds and made investment recommendations on real estate purchases and participating loans. One of the key measures of financial feasibility was the internal rate of return (IRR). One of the pension funds began to comment that our project IRRs were less than what other advisers were showing. They finally said that, unless we could improve our IRRs, they would be inclined to do fewer investments with us.

We looked at our deals. They did not seem much different from what was happening in the market. Finally, I looked at how our IRR was calculated. Aha! Our IRR was calculated on an annual basis, and we made the assumption that the return for any given year came in at the end of the year. What if you changed the assumption to the beginning of the year? What if you moved the sale of the investment up to the last year of the analysis, not the year after? We tested these options.

The increase in our IRRs was dramatic, and it placed us back in the ballpark of our esteemed competitors. We followed up with several of our competitors and found that they actually did their IRRs on a monthly basis, not annually. Still, this was a significant improvement over our old practice. We changed to monthly, and our customer called several months later to congratulate us on our obviously improved deal-making skills, as our returns were now comparable to the competition. We said, "Thank you," and left it at that.

> **PEARL OF WISDOM:**
> *After using these sophisticated measurements, we became believers in The KISS Principle: Keep it Simple, Stupid. Do not overthink analytics. Today, return on cost is our preferred analytical measurement. Using our savings account example, it would be 5 percent. If you are buying a stock, it would be the dividend divided by the stock price. That is all there should be to analytics.*

Let nonanalytic analysis decide about growth prospects and relevant industry factors, and listen to your all-important gut feel. In your non-real estate business, the analytics most likely will be your gross margin (revenue divided by cost) and your NTM. The definition of NTM is towards the end of the chapter.

How does this apply to your business? In real estate, yields (also known as "returns") vary based on product type, location, and curb appeal. Currently, apartments are the most desired and have the lowest relative return in the real estate world. Industrial buildings are next in line, with retail, office, and hotels far behind. These positions change over time. In a normal environment, an apartment project might require a yield premium of 2 percent, known in the industry as two hundred basis points, over a comparable ten-year US Treasury yield. For retail and office, the spread is more in the 4–5 percent range.

This would be relatively easy to figure out if you were dealing with the state of the market as it is today. Unfortunately, if you are developing a new business line or a real estate project, the appropriate metric is when the product or project is built and ready for the consumer to buy in four to five years. This situation is the same as when you start your business and project revenue and expenses five years into the future. Your non-analytic side hopes that the economy will not take a nosedive as you ramp up.

How does a business leader figure out what the yield needs to be five years from now to have a successful product, and to make a profit? How do you plan for disruptions and uncertainty?

Many years ago, a real estate study was conducted to look at this issue from a different perspective. When the project is built, leased, and ready for permanent financing, or sale, the financing and sales markets may range from great to terrible.

This is like the joke about two hikers seeing a grizzly bear rambling toward them. One starts to run while the other bends over to tie his sneakers. The first says, "Why aren't you running?" The second says, "I don't have to outrun the bear, I only have to outrun you." The different perspective, like the joke, was meant to consider the situation not in the absolute, but relative to the rest of the market in the future.

At the time of the study, for office development, it was decided that a 12 percent yield or return on cost (the annual return divided by the total cost of the project) would place the project in the top quartile of projects being financed or sold in almost any given time period. In a favorable market, it would be easy to get financing or sell. In a normal market, you can obtain the financing or sale on acceptable terms, and in an unfavorable or high-interest rate market, a 12 percent return on cost would make the project one of the few that can be financed or sold at a profit.

Think of that "banker's window." How high must my return be to feel confident that the window will be open and receptive when I step up five years from now?

The benchmark return on cost for our projects was 12 percent. We made elaborate ten-year Excel spreadsheets. Fancy investment metrics like IRR and net present value (NPV) were calculated, but at the end of the day, this simple measurement of return on cost became the most trustworthy evaluation tool.

Commercial real estate has many different analytic metrics. Practitioners of the art often tend to go back and forth between metrics, talking in an unrecognizable code.

One night at dinner, while I was pontificating on these analytics, my wife asked, "What's my NTM?"

"NTM? Never heard of that. We don't use it," I said.

She replied, "Come on, Chris. It's very straightforward. I'm sure you know what it is."

Professing ignorance, I requested the definition of NTM.

NTM: "Net To Me." How much is in my checkbook after this project comes online and gets financed?

What was there to say? She was absolutely correct. To this day, NTM is the preferred metric used in this household for both real estate and other investments.

> **PEARL OF WISDOM:**
> *NTM applies to your business.*
> *It is not a real estate measurement. Just ask your significant other.*

Of course, NTM does not appear in any real estate analysis textbook, and you will not find its acronym on any computer or calculator tab. Several years after this epiphany, the Urban Land Institute had a course on real estate finance. The ULI, as mentioned earlier, is one of the premier industry organizations and a continuing source of expertise and intelligence. Think Lifetime Learning, one of the keys to success.

The professor asked if I would do a ULI session on analytics and returns. At that time, the standard handheld calculator was an HP 12C, which had tabs for various real estate analytics. We worked our way through the tabs and then, as you would expect, the final analytic, NTM, was introduced. Students frantically searched their calculators for the correct tab, which, of course, was not there. In the back, the professor began to worry. After soaking the moment for as much drama as possible, the true meaning of NTM was revealed. Everyone thought it was funny and appropriate, except for the professor, who was not at all amused.

That 12 percent number is now probably closer to 10 percent, as long-term treasury yields have been at rock bottom for the past ten years. This has led to the tendency for developers (and business owners) to become complacent, and assume that lower rates of return will be feasible five years out. Part of the current (2024) malaise in business is that long term treasury yields have increased rapidly by almost 3%. Many new business ventures were planned five years ago with returns that are now too low. Entrepreneurs are feeling the squeeze as they try to improve yields in this rising rate environment with a teller window that is basically closed.

Several years ago, many developers decided to get into the apartment business, seeing that they could build to a 6 percent return on cost and sell at a 4 percent return. At one ULI meeting, our group was polled and approximately 70 percent of the group was building apartments for sale. A year later, the same group was polled, and virtually no one was building apartments for sale. What happened? During the prior twelve months, the 4 percent return had climbed to 5.5 percent with the strong possibility of going above 6 percent. Most of our group managed to sell their apartments at better than a six, and while they did not make as much money as they hoped, they did not lose money. It was a reminder that you must measure your feasibility against long-term trends and not short-term conditions.

The most perilous situation occurs in business when long-term interest rates rise, production costs increase, and sales prices stagnate, putting downward pressure on the return on cost. In these circumstances, many business ventures and real estate projects become financially unfeasible. Depending on how far along the project is, this could be disastrous. It is why real estate developers are hesitant to inventory land or participate in projects with long predevelopment periods, where the risk of interest rate fluctuations is high.

This leads to a short discussion on how to manage this risk. Clearly, if one makes a five-year bet on the direction of interest rates, the ability to manage the risk is paramount. The most straightforward way to manage risk in this environment as a real estate developer is to not buy the land, but to option it for a long enough period to obtain all the entitlements, firm up cost estimates, find financing, and have a good feel for the market before starting construction. An "option" is buying the right to purchase something at a specific time and price in the future, but not being obligated to buy. Occasionally it is also possible to tie down interest rate costs through hedges, swaps, or forward fixed-rate loan commitments. These risk mitigation efforts have a cost, but the cost is a fair price to pay, given the risk that is being avoided or laid off.

If it takes five years to go from the gleam in the eye to the finished product, those five years generally comprise one to two years to design the product, tie up the land, and get the necessary building permits and governmental approvals; twelve to eighteen months to bring the product to market; and another twelve months to reach the desired levels of leasing revenue. With the risk window reduced from five years to two, managing the risk becomes much easier.

CHAPTER 8
PERSONNEL

Employees Are Smart. Listen To Them.

People: another unfortunate necessity for growing a company. Having the right people in the right spot at the right time, contrary to the prior sentence, is a very fortunate and rewarding part of growing a company. They are the teammates who share your goals and aspirations. The men and women who go on to start their own companies are successful because of what they learned while with your company. The key parts of the personnel equation are people management, leadership, and listening.

PEOPLE MANAGEMENT

Going back to Jack's Pearl of Wisdom observations about strengths and weaknesses (page 22), Pete and I shared one glaring weakness: human resources. Having a human resources person in-house was always an unnecessary luxury. McGill Development Company was small. What need was there for a human resources person? While the company may have not needed an in-house human resources person, it became evident that it needed the expertise. One of our mentors pointed out that the company seemed to be running at a subpar level. He thought the issue was our mix of employees, and he recommended a specific consultant.

The consultant interviewed every person in the company, including us, and came back with this unbelievable, but true, observation. The problem was at the top: It was us. Our weakness was that we believed everybody else worked the same way we did, with entrepreneurial zeal and a strong work ethic. He revealed that not everybody worked that way. There is a group of people who are more interested in gaming the system, taking advantage of other people's willingness to help, and taking credit for other people's achievements, and in the process, undermining the enterprise. We were clueless. The consultant identified four people in the company who behaved this way, and we let them go. It made a huge, positive difference.

Going forward, the rule was that any prospective employee would be interviewed by the consultant. He had the final veto. Shortly after all this happened, we interviewed people for a position. The interviews went well, and only one interview remained. The consultant did his interview in about fifteen minutes and vetoed the hire. One of our employees disagreed and voiced her concern. He responded that she would be the one to call up the prospect and tell them they were not being hired.

Before the call, he explained: "This person will be your best friend if you do exactly what she wants you to do. But the moment you refuse to do as she wants, she will turn on you and become an enemy."

She made the call. The prospect lashed out at our employee and hung up on her. Our employee's first question was, "How did you know?" He said, "I have interviewed thousands and thousands of people over my career, and I easily can spot behavior that will be detrimental to the company."

After that, no one ever questioned his veto.

Christopher W. Kurz

On a broader level, building on Jack's observations on strengths and weaknesses, it is imperative to identify not just personal weaknesses but corporate weaknesses and to build expertise to address these weaknesses. Following up on our experience with human resources, we circled back to all the company vendors, had a strength-weakness conversation with them, and asked them to be vigilant on our behalf in the areas we might need help. It made a big difference.

Your passion most likely will lead to building an organization that needs human resources. In biotech, it is standard to bring human resources expertise on board when founders start hiring. The biotech business is labor intensive, and hiring the right people in the right place is a key to success. Your business is probably more akin to biotech than real estate. A word to the wise.

LEADERSHIP

Leadership happens both in your company and in your industry. Industry leadership can be a key ingredient in opening doors to more rapid growth for your company.

As a full-time developer, the Mortgage Bankers Association relationship gave way to the Urban Land Institute. ULI is an international, multidisciplinary nonprofit comprised of developers, architects, lawyers, bankers, public officials, and just about anyone else involved in real estate. One of the unique aspects of ULI is that if you, as a member, are asked a question, it is expected that the question will be answered fully and honestly. No secrets. This played out at a national meeting in Boston, where two Orange County, California, office developers described the competition for a tenant. They bared their souls. Afterward, one of them said his competitor probably already knew everything he had said.

At a meeting early in the life of the company in Philadelphia, Pete and I spotted the San Jose developer who had pioneered the development of flex buildings. WHY NOT US time. He generously gave us half an hour on the spot to talk about what he thought was important in the development of flex buildings. We were blown away.

ULI became an important part of creating an identity in the development world, and an invaluable resource when working out seemingly insurmountable problems. It also was my main conduit for lifetime learning and gaining stature in the industry.

In order to be the best, it is beneficial to learn from the best. Penn, Wharton, and Rouse were among the best. Attending semiannual ULI national meetings, and rising to leadership in the organization, created the perfect environment for continuing education. Other ULI leaders were the stars of the industry. Being around them and being able to talk with them, comparing notes, and seeking advice was invaluable.

One of the detriments of being local is being a fish in a small pond. There are no big fish in small ponds. The big fish on the national and international stage have little time for small fish. How can a small fish swim with big fish? Becoming a leader in a national industry organization is one way. With patience and time spent leading at the local level, the big fish began to take notice. The ULI designation that allowed me to swim with the big fish was an appointment as a ULI Trustee. Being selected as a Trustee was a great personal honor. This small fish from Baltimore could now swim in the larger waters among the big fish.

Being a ULI Trustee also gave credibility to the company's sophistication and skill level. The company was automatically deemed worthy of investment and notice. A small fish that could now swim with the big fish.

LISTENING

PEARL OF WISDOM:
Listen and be open-minded. It is surprising what you learn.

Both of our children played youth baseball. When Tim was in the eleven to thirteen age bracket on the Cavaliers, I volunteered to help his coach, who was also named Chris. Coach Chris was a young lawyer with an infant daughter and no kids on the team. I was happy to do whatever he needed. When Tim turned fourteen, Coach Chris called with the schedule for the coming season. I pointed out that Tim was too old for the Cavaliers. His immediate response was to say that he was calling me, not Tim, and did I have any questions about the schedule. So began a seventeen-year tenure as an assistant coach on the Cavaliers. The only caveat was that, if my presence prevented a Cavalier parent from helping out, I would step aside for that parent.

Over seventeen years, the Cavaliers were league champs about half the time. How were we able to do that? At the beginning of each season, Coach Chris would enumerate our three goals: have fun, make new friends, and become better baseball players. No mention of winning. Parents, players, and coaches were not allowed to say anything derogatory to another team member or an opposing player. No tolerance.

Remember Jack's Pearl of Wisdom? The secret to the team's success was to teach the fundamentals of baseball to every kid on the team and to help them become better players, especially the weaker ones. Out of fourteen kids on the team, three or four usually were very good. The coaches could make them a little better, but not enough to make a real difference. The needle really moved up when the other players got better. The worse a player was at the beginning, the greater their impact on the team as the season progressed. This makes weakness a strength!

Coach Chris had two daughters, Claire and Maureen, who played on the Cavaliers. Maureen asked if her friend, Serena, could join the team. Of course, she could. Serena had recently arrived from Pakistan and knew absolutely nothing about baseball. But she was athletic and game to learn. During her first time up at bat, she swung at three wild pitches, struck out, and came back to the bench, clearly frustrated.

"Serena, did we talk to you about the strike zone?"

"No, what's that?"

This was a coaching mistake. We explained the strike zone, and she replied that now things were starting to make sense. By the end of the season, she was a pretty good baseball player.

Christopher W. Kurz

Claire was going up to bat. I said, "If you hit a home run, you can drive my Porsche."

Why did I say that? Because Claire had never hit a home run, and I assumed she could not. Claire hit a sharp grounder toward the second baseman, and she hustled down to first. The ball went right between the fielder's legs and out into right field. Claire headed to second, and you could tell what was on her mind. The right fielder picked up the ball and froze as multiple fielders called for the ball. Around third base came Claire, steaming toward home plate. As she crossed the plate for a home run, she yelled to me, "You promised!" I promptly paid up.

Zach was the type of kid you can picture at a piano recital and not playing baseball. He did not appear athletic and could barely throw the ball more than twenty feet. At the first practice, his mom came up to the coaches and proffered that Zach could pitch. We were polite, but did not see any merit in trying Zach on the pitching mound. At the second practice, Mom was more insistent that her son could pitch. Finally, she intoned that Zach had taken pitching lessons. To mollify Mom, Zach was asked if he wanted to try out for pitcher. To our amazement, he said, "Yes."

Zach stood on the mound and did a funky, unorthodox wind-up, and fired a perfect fastball to the catcher. Turned out that while Zach could not throw to first base, he could really, really pitch.

The best part of the Zach story was the opening game of the season. When the opposing players saw who was pitching for the Cavaliers, they were unmerciful in their teasing. After they batted in the first inning, there was not a word from their side. Zach was happy. The coaches were happy. But the happiest person at the game was Zach's Mom.

PEARL OF WISDOM
Do not assume a person cannot do something. Give them a chance to do it. You will be surprised.

This story is about listening to those who you may think have little to say to you.

As the business grew, the company also grew, adding a head of construction and in-house leasing talent. On the leasing front, a young man was hired out of college based on a strong recommendation. Steve was from Bel Air, Maryland. Bel Air is a medium-sized town approximately twenty miles northeast of Baltimore. Bel Air was not on the radar screen for development, though this young man kept promoting its promise.

One Friday morning, Steve asked me to lunch after having checked the desk calendar to make sure the lunch hour was free. Instead of going to a local eatery in Columbia, he headed us north to Bel Air, determined to give his hometown proper consideration. Up I-95 Steve drove through the Fort McHenry tunnel and on up towards Wilmington to new Route 24, which connects the I-95 Interstate to the town of Bel Air, ten miles to the northwest.

Route 24 was bordered on both sides by new developments. It looked like Southern California, not at all what I expected.

The intersection between Route 24 and Route 1 is the major retail district in the region with over sixty thousand cars passing through per day. The four quadrants of the intersection consisted of a Sears/Macy's regional mall, a Kmart/Giant Food anchored power center, and a thirty-year-old neighborhood shopping center anchored by an Acme grocery store.

The fourth quadrant was an eight-acre pasture populated by Betsy and her fellow cows. It was owned by the estate of Mr. Deaton, who had been the town surveyor and had been uninterested in selling his farm for development. The eight-acre site was not zoned for retail use and had not been incorporated into the town. It would require rezoning to be developed. Further down Route 24 and back toward I-95 was a thirty-acre site with superb access and retail zoning.

At this point, you are probably wondering how our corporate metrics could possibly be bent to fit either one of these projects into the pipeline. The Toombs Rule of Real Estate did not fit. Neither one of these sites was conducive to mixed-use development. These were the guardrails along the business road, which kept McGill from veering off into the gutter of mediocrity. Like the sirens of Greek mythology, these two locations called out for us to abandon all that had been learned previously.

A study of the retail markets in the Bel Air region showed that no new retail had been built in probably ten years and that the existing retail had significant functional obsolescence. With the construction of Route 24, the Bel Air area had become much more attractive as a residential suburb to Baltimore. The residential population was growing rapidly.

The larger tract was owned by two individuals who had bought up numerous tracts of land in anticipation of Route 24. The daughter of one was a classmate of our daughter in school, so there was an opening for a conversation. This site also drew the attention of numerous other large retail developers. At the end of the day, the site was sold to Trammell Crow, a large national developer from Texas, in part due to the seller's excitement in doing a deal with a large developer with such a fantastic reputation. Goliath beat David this time.

Through Steve's contacts as a hometown boy, it was possible to meet with the executor of the Deaton estate. The estate owned the eight-acre cow farm. The analysis of the Route 24/Route One intersection was that there were approximately two million square feet of existing retail space. All the desirable anchor tenants were already at the intersection. The retail space for smaller tenants tended to be poorly located, with deep store depths of over 120 feet. None of the current crop of desirable small-store retailers were in Bel Air. The product differentiation strategy was to build small-store space with depths of only sixty to a hundred feet. It would thus be successfully differentiated on a nonmonetary basis. With no need for an anchor tenant with a low rent, long-term lease, it was possible to pay a premium price for the land. Soon afterward, we signed an agreement with the executor of the estate.

As mentioned, the site was not incorporated into the town of Bel Air or zoned for retail. In Maryland, the prevalent political jurisdiction is a county. In a limited number of counties, there are also incorporated cities and towns. In these areas, real estate pays both the county real estate tax and city/town real estate tax. When the other three quadrants of the intersection were developed, they were required to be incorporated into the town. From a public policy perspective, this made sense, as it helped provide the town with a greater tax base. This site would be no exception.

The process involved first, to apply for rezoning in the county, which would be denied, and then to apply to be incorporated into the town with the requisite retail zoning. There were no guarantees that the site would be zoned for retail.

Before applying to rezone, it is customary to meet with the neighboring communities for their input. At the community meeting, an individual showed up wearing a dirty T-shirt and matching jeans. He pointed to the site plan and his house across from the site on Kelly Avenue. This street bordered the site going from Route One back into the residential neighborhood. He wanted to know if there was any way that Kelly Avenue could be modified to become an entrance to the shopping center, but no longer be a road into the neighborhood. It sounded like a good idea. The site engineer was invited into the conversation and drew a possible solution that satisfied the young man. The site plan was changed.

On the night of the zoning hearing, the town hall was packed to overflowing. After squeezing into the main meeting room and finding our attorney, I asked, "Who are all these people, and are they here to oppose our plan?" The attorney did not know.

The Bel Air Town Center petition was first up. The site engineers made their presentation, and the town planning office recommended approval. It was time for community input.

An elderly gentleman shuffled out of the crowd. Our attorney identified him as Mr. Brown, managing partner of Brown, Brown, and Brown, the oldest law firm in town, and one of the neighbors. This did not look good. Mr. Brown stepped to the microphone.

The crowd was hushed.

Mr. Brown just had one question. He noted that Kelly Avenue would no longer go back into his neighborhood, but would make a left-hand turn into the shopping center. Was this a correct reading of the plan? The planning staff confirmed that his reading was correct.

Mr. Brown then opined that the neighborhood had been trying for years to close Kelly Avenue, and it looked like, finally, this developer was going to make it happen. That being the case, he and the neighborhood recommended immediate approval of our shopping center and the closing of Kelly Avenue.

The planning board chair thanked Mr. Brown for his testimony, and in one long sentence, called for any other commentary, finding none, closed the discussion and moved for approval, which was immediately granted.

The question remained: Who were all these people, and why were they at the meeting?

The second item up at the town hall meeting was for the approval of another retail site not too far from ours. It was owned by a defunct savings and loan, which had made promises to the neighborhood that had not been fulfilled. The crowd hanging from the rafters was there to ensure no zoning approval would be granted until those promises were fulfilled. That zoning request was denied.

PEARL OF WISDOM:
The Pearls of Wisdom learned?
Listen to your young employ-
ees. Never mistake the appearance of the

messenger for the message. Always have the site engineer at a public meeting. Going first is always best.

The executor asked if the cows could be a part of the sale. No way. At the start of construction, a hundred years of accumulated topsoil was piled in one corner of the site.

The next morning, a cross appeared on the top of the pile inscribed with: "Here lies Betsy." The humor was appreciated, and Betsy reappeared as a life-sized paper mache cow at the grand opening.

At that time, the financial markets were favorable. Financial institutions from outside the region established loan production offices and were eager for new business. Crossland Savings Bank from Brooklyn, New York, had opened a loan production office headed by a local banker who knew us well. They were happy to make a construction loan to McGill with no other financial partners.

Fellow entrepreneurs, you will understand what a monumental achievement this was. No financial partners!

Steve was delighted he would get to lease this project in his hometown. He set his sights on the Tex-Mex restaurant chain, Chili's. Chili's is owned by Brinker, a national restaurant company. The standard operating procedure for doing a market analysis for a retail site is to look at census data within a prescribed driving radius of the location. We used local housing and income data to update the 1980 census. This would only work if we could convince the head of real estate that these numbers made more sense than the conventional approach. Steve was merciless and hounded the Chili's head of real estate until this gentleman finally told Steve that he would come to Bel Air for half a day and that when he turned down the site, Steve would agree to never, ever call him again.

The gentleman came, and Steve, using all his local boy charm, took him around town, ending at lunch at the only restaurant remotely comparable to Chili's. They had lunch, and the gentleman told Steve that Chili's would come to the site. The opening was the best opening the restaurant had experienced to date in the United States. Its first-year operating results put the Bel Air location in the top ten nationally.

In retrospect, this was partially a function of the population growth in the area, but also the fact that there was no competition. Chili's was the first of what would prove to be many national restaurant chains coming to the intersection. Upon receiving their first-year sales, Steve called to congratulate Chili's. Their response was to say thank you for the congratulations, but they did not expect this to continue. If sales cooled off, Chili's would still be happy with this site. They expected their competition to all show up in the next four years, which they did.

Despite breaking all the rules and the guardrails, Bel Air Town Center proved to be a tremendous success. It would be nice to say that guardrails are only suggestions, but the reality is, this was truly a unique location, and McGill's retail leasing experience and expertise made the project a success. Lady Luck also played a big role. Later the guardrails were ignored on another shopping center project that was not successful—disregard guardrails at your peril. Lucky once does not mean lucky always.

THE VANISHING ART OF FACE-TO-FACE MEETING PSYCHOLOGY

With the onset of work at home, meeting psychology is quickly becoming a lost art. This is a continuation of the impact of Microsoft Word and computer editing on business negotiations. Twenty years ago, business negotiations were done face-to-face. You learned to read body language and voice inflections as indicators of what the other side was truly after. Today you just receive the next draft by email with changes marked in a different color. It is harder to figure out where the middle ground is. Talking by phone helps communicate one's position, but the color is lost. Impasses usually require a meeting. Now meetings are by Zoom and the "last option," a face-to-face meeting, is becoming obsolete.

The face-to-face meeting, along with the handwritten note, is now a business strategy itself, designed not to negotiate a deal, but to develop a rapport with the folks you will be doing business with. Before we all forget how to benefit from these meetings, and a well-handwritten note, the following are some observations on meetings. Not precisely Pearls of Wisdoms, but good to know.

The purpose of a meeting dictates the psychology.

If the objective is warmth, encouragement, or praise, arrange the meeting in a comfortable, living-room-like setting. If you are the lead, make sure everyone can easily see your face and read your mood. This communicates that you are serious in your messaging.

If the meeting is all business, gather around a table so people can take notes. If you want lots of input, sit in the middle of the table, not at the end. If you do not want lots of input, sit at the end in the position of authority.

If you are meeting just one person and want the position of authority, put a piece of furniture between the two of you, generally your desk if you have your own office. If you want cooperation and input, make sure the space between you and them is open—no furniture.

If you want the meeting to be quick, do it while standing up.

If you are meeting on someone else's turf, try to sit with your back to a window. It is much easier to read a person's face and body language if they are facing the light. It is hard to do this if you are fighting the glare.

Never, ever take a phone call during a meeting. Turn your phone off. Aside from being rude, it signals that this meeting is not that important to you.

Always, always be on time. Early is better. Being late is saying that you do not value the other person's time. Once in my career, I was busy and always ran late. I was not managing my time well. It was not pretty. The answer was to tell the meeting participants at the beginning of the meeting when I had to leave. I gave a five-minute warning and at the designated time got up to leave. The initial reaction was, "But we're not finished."

I would say, "My time is up. I told you so. I will not keep the next meeting waiting." Like training a puppy, it took a few times, but eventually, people honored my schedule, especially when I was no longer late for their meeting.

CHAPTER 9
BUSINESS STRATEGIES AND CULTURE

The culture you establish has a profound impact on company strategy and performance, positive or negative. As discussed in the finance chapter, the type of business often dictates the best culture.

Sometimes you think you have found the perfect embodiment of your corporate culture. Many years ago in Kyoto, Japan, I saw and bought this Japanese woodblock print.

To my Western eyes, the figure was a Samurai warrior and the embodiment of an entrepreneur: aggressive, humble, relentless, and passionate. A real Why Not Me person. It has been in my office ever since and served as a continuing source of inspiration. This is the type of company we want to be. This is our culture.

There has been recent research on the artist and subject matter. The 1794 print is of Kabuki actor Otani Oniji III as Yakko Edobei in the play, *The Colored Reins of a Loving Wife*. The artist is Toshusai Sharaku.

Little did I realize what any person familiar with Kabuki theater would know—Yakko Edobei is no Japanese samurai warrior. He is a ruthless, wicked manservant, a real "bad guy" in a famous Japanese play. He is certainly not a representation of good entrepreneurial characteristics. Maybe I should have looked harder at the print. Maybe I should have done some research. I look back and laugh at myself. The print certainly has served its intended purpose, but it is now a commentary on taking something out of its cultural context and completely misunderstanding what it is. A mistake made, lesson learned going forward.

> **PEARL OF WISDOM:**
> *Make sure your perception of the culture is the same as that of your employees and the public. Fortunately, Yakko Edobei never made it out of my office.*

PROMOTING A WIN-WIN CULTURE

One of the basic premises of a successful business strategy is understanding the needs of the people on the other side of the table. Your efforts to give them what they need will help you get what you need.

> **PEARL OF WISDOM:**
> *A Pearl of Wisdom from our lawyer is that in any legal negotiation, the other side must have about 25 percent of what is negotiated, and you need the same. The remaining 50 percent most likely will not matter and can be conceded to obtain what you need. The key is to know what the other side must have. Our lawyer, Neil, always knew what both parties needed,*

and when the other party's lawyer realized this, we quickly came to a final agreement. In one negotiation, Neil declared a bathroom break to pull me aside and tell me to stop negotiating. We had all that we needed. We went back into the room and said we had no more issues. The other side felt the same way, and the deal was done.

PEARL OF WISDOM:
You will often run into someone who does not believe in a win-win scenario. They view life as a zero-sum game. For them to "win," you must also "lose." For them, it is not enough to have their 25 percent. They must have as much of your 25 percent as they can get, plus the remaining 50 percent. This should cause a red flag to go off in your brain. Such behavior does not stop when the deal is signed. Indeed, in their view, the legal document is merely a set of suggestions that they are free to ignore. Doing business with this sort is not worth it, period. Been there, done that. I hope it never happens to you.

Below are a few examples of corporate culture and how their culture impacted their future. While the companies are in real estate, the Pearls of Wisdom's are universal.

THE ROUSE COMPANY

The Rouse Company was led by James Rouse, a legendary entrepreneur in real estate. The company culture was highly entrepreneurial. In addition to developing the new town of Columbia, Maryland, The Rouse Company was also one of the leading regional mall developers in the country. For me, a graduate school summer job became full-time upon graduation. Part of the summer assignment was to work on "grand opening" marketing campaigns for new regional malls. Interestingly, all these marketing campaigns were targeted toward communicating the unique "experience" the consumer would receive, a concept way ahead of its time in commercial real estate.

PEARL OF WISDOM:
It's only after I was at Penn, Wharton, and The Rouse Company, that I realized these three incredible entities provided a fantastic start to a business career. The Pearl of Wisdom is that, as you begin your career, always try to associate with the very best. They will give you the best education, academically and in the field, which will make you the best entrepreneur you can be.

The Rouse Company had an analytics group that did the economic models for all its projects. It was a great place to start and provided great exposure to the company's development projects. This was a long time ago. Dial-up modems, rudimentary programming, and reams of paper were the norm. The concept of a computer screen was yet to arrive. In the context of WHY NOT ME, this job played to my analytical strengths, which would become a primary part of my business repertoire.

At some point, the regional mall development group needed additional manpower, and the opportunity arose to move from the analytical group to the regional mall development group. This move provided the opportunity to completely pursue my passion for commercial real estate development in a highly entrepreneurial environment. It was truly the training ground for what was to come.

Learning to write made a cameo appearance when it came time to write the first proposal to an outside company. The division chief insisted on reviewing the letter. It came back with more red ink than black.

PEARL OF WISDOM:
The most glaring mistake was the use of pronouns. There are no pronouns in business correspondence. This letter was not from an individual, but was from the company outlining the terms of a potential long-term department store lease. Any use of pronouns was unnecessary and unprofessional.

Back to the drawing board. It was much more difficult to rewrite the letter as instructed, but the result was a much more compact and professional letter. Henceforth, I would write all correspondence in the same way. It made, and continues to make, a big difference in the success of presentations, proposals, and day-to-day written correspondence. A Pearl of Wisdom.

I would like to point out that this dictum of not using pronouns does not apply to writing books! The initial drafts of this book adhered to the no-pronoun principle. Every reader of the drafts commented that the stories would have more punch and meaning if I would just loosen up and tell them in the first person. I have tried.

The Rouse Company was known for its entrepreneurial culture, in large part, due to its founder, James Rouse. This was evident on a trip with him to Atlanta for a morning speaking engagement with an Atlanta business group.

The night before, there was a dinner with Jim Rouse, Dick Rich, Chairman of Rich's Department Stores, Alvin Ferst, his executive vice president, the head of Central Atlanta Progress, and his number two, Dick Fleming (the same Wharton dorm counselor who recommended Rouse to me).

Toward the end of dinner, the talk turned to politics. Richard Nixon had just been reelected President, but Watergate was not yet in the news. Jim Rouse opined that Nixon would not finish his term as President. This got the immediate attention of Dick Rich, who asked Jim to repeat what he said and why he thought so. Rouse responded that he knew nothing about how this might happen, but that he thought Nixon's persona and behavior were such that the American public would not tolerate him for four more years. Impressed, Rich asked Rouse if he would like to wager some money on that outcome. Rouse immediately agreed to bet $100 that Nixon would not finish his term. Rich took the bet.

As a twenty-seven-year-old who had never seen a $100 bill, this seemed otherworldly. Here was the head of the company saying an outlandish thing to one of our most important customers, and he was willing to put money on his opinion. He was nuts!

Of course, Jim Rouse's prediction came to pass. He was right. Nixon did resign. The day after the resignation, Rouse received a $100 wire from Dick Rich.

The Pearls of Wisdom from this dinner were three.

Jim Rouse had the ability to think forward and outside the box, even if his conclusions seemed unthinkable. The essence of being an entrepreneur. Rouse had absolute faith in how he saw life, both in politics and business (PW 1). Furthermore, he was willing to wager serious money. He put his money, and the firm's, behind his beliefs (PW 2). The third takeaway was the $100 wire from Dick Rich. Rouse did not call, nothing was in writing, and Rich could have ignored the bet, but Rich sent a wire for $100 within twenty-four hours. As impressive as Rouse's Pearls of Wisdom were, Mr. Rich's Pearl was also. If you are a man of your word, act that way. This is why Claire got her ride in the Porsche.

Rouse had a project in Toronto, Sherway Gardens Mall, which was being expanded. Summoned to his office, the boss indicated to me that all was not well in Toronto. It was October and the project had to open by Memorial Day. It looked to be over budget, but no one was sure. The project was 15 percent leased and needed to be 25 percent leased to qualify for the next construction loan draw. I was off to Toronto to assess the situation and figure out how to fix things.

It was bad. Very bad. The project was two million dollars over budget. In retail leasing, there is a line item for tenant concessions, generally in the form of a tenant improvement allowance. As the project was only 15 percent lease, this budget was largely unspent. It went to cover the construction cost overruns.

This was Rouse's first international project. In the U.S., the in-house leasing team negotiated leases and worked with the legal department to sign them. In Toronto, for some unknown reason, Rouse was using a (very good) local retail broker instead of the in-house group.

At the first meeting with the leasing brokers, I was ready to lean hard into their shortcomings and lack of leasing. Before I could start, they dropped a fat file on the table filled with letters of intent, agreed to by prospective tenants, but languishing because no one knew what to do with them. No one realized there was a gap in the process—no conduit between the broker and the legal department. Into the breach I went, converting letters of intent (LOI's) into signed leases. In the ensuing six months, as LOI's were converted to leases, negotiated, and signed, I learned more about leasing and real estate development than in the prior four years.

At five every evening, there was a conference call with the Rouse legal department back in Columbia to go over, explain, and resolve legal issues on pending leases. The next morning, it was back on the phone with prospective tenants and the broker to finalize the deal. Sherway Gardens was successful, and there were no shortage of prospects. As soon as the local broker saw the log jam break, they were off to the races improving the quality of prospects. The expansion opened on time, on budget, 85 percent leased with rents over pro forma.

Why tell this story? For all the wonderful aspects of The Rouse Company, there was a cultural arrogance that made it desirable to do the perfect deal rather than just do the deal. Major deals languished over minutia. There was no urgency. It almost killed the company.

One of the major lessons learned from Rouse was the importance of being fast, humble, and relentless in transacting business. One of the popular clichés in this business is that "time kills all deals," and this is very true. My six months in Toronto were an invaluable education. As your business grows and gains plaudits and acclaim, it is important to remain true to your passion and stay fast, humble, and relentless.

Christopher W. Kurz

BUSINESS GROWTH AT MCGILL:
TO SCALE OR NOT TO SCALE

Once an entrepreneur has successfully launched their enterprise, the business strategy question eventually arises: How big should the enterprise be? In many businesses, once the base business model has proven successful, it is logical to scale the business, grow geographically, and expand the product offering. Generally, the enterprise also has investors expecting the business to scale. It is also not unusual at some point in time for the investors to decide that the founder (you!) needs to be replaced with management more adept at managing a large enterprise. This is especially true if aspirational financial targets are missed.

If your goal is to maintain control of the enterprise, growing can be more difficult, but not impossible.

In the real estate world, investors are property-specific. Retaining control of your company is not difficult, but at the property level, the risks are as described in the finance chapter. A disgruntled investor can usually force the sale of the property. As the enterprise grows, it is best to remember that properties and investors may come and go.

Baltimore is thirty-five miles north of Washington, DC. By comparison, Washington is a major-league real estate town with almost every national developer and many institutions doing business. Baltimore is a minor-league town with no national developers and only an occasional institutional investor. There are advantages to being in the minor leagues, especially if the company has some major-league skills. But the siren call to play with the big boys is enticing. After the company was established, we spent a fair amount of time looking in the District of Columbia, Montgomery County, and Northern Virginia for acquisitions and development opportunities. A joint venture to buy an office complex with an institutional investor morphed into a brokerage fee as the price rose too high. In general, the increased competition in Washington lowered returns below McGill's risk-adjusted threshold.

Washington has a thriving land speculation business that does not exist in Baltimore. Several times the company considered dirt opportunities held by speculators. The speculators knew their basis was too high for development but hoped to foist their land off on the next speculator.

At some point, reality settled in that, as exciting as the Washington real estate scene was, it was not an arena that would be profitable for McGill. So, it was back to Baltimore with higher yields, less competition, no land speculators, and embracing the culture of a local business.

This experience led to a reassessment of the strengths and objectives. Thanks to WHY NOT US, product differentiation, the Toombs Rule of Real Estate, several Pearls of Wisdom, and a fresh look at strengths and weaknesses, it was clear that it was best for us to stay local and focus on Baltimore submarkets that had sufficient demand to support large-scale, mixed-use real estate projects. These submarkets turned out to be on the south side of town in the Baltimore-Washington corridor.

A nice aspect of this type of commercial real estate is that one does not need many successes to have great personal financial gains. You could remain small and control your destiny, but you could still get rich.

There was also another cultural factor: work/life balance. Both Pete and I had spent part of our careers as road warriors—living on airplanes, leaving home on Mondays and returning on Fridays.

It sounded exciting, but it sucked. Aside from our work passions, our families were also a major passion. The ability to control the work schedule and make the kid's games and performances was more important than being in San Francisco. Back then, everyone had paper calendars that sat on the desk. Secretaries could book meetings by looking at the calendar. If the calendar's owner booked something, it was their responsibility to put it on the calendar. There was a code at McGill that we used to indicate a family event. This meant nothing could be scheduled that might interfere with the family event. Why the code? Sometimes someone would insist that they meet at a particular time, and the calendar *had* to be changed. Business meetings could be rescheduled to accommodate this, but not a family event. No exceptions.

LINDEN ASSOCIATES, INC.

After the 1990 recession and the demise of McGill, Linden Associates, Inc. was formed in 1992 as a mortgage brokerage and real estate development company. Initial revenues came from brokering mortgages to familiar lenders for borrowers primarily in the mid-Atlantic. It was a reprise of my mortgage banking experience, only not with an employer, a paycheck, or a fancy downtown office. The business strategy was twofold—mortgage banking as a sturdy foundation in the service side of the business and development for its wealth creation. The McGill total reliance on real estate development was to be avoided. Personnel would be added only when desperately needed.

Bill Rouse was right about planning for better times.

Merritt was able to restructure its finances with the bank. They gave back the AT&T properties to the bank with a right of first refusal to match any offer the bank should receive on the properties. On a Friday, Merritt received a certified letter from the bank indicating they had an offer to sell the AT&T parcels to a local investor, who was a big client of the bank. Merritt had one week to exercise the right of first refusal and post a $250,000 deposit. By sheer fate, Pete had dinner Sunday night with Leroy and learned of this development. Also, by sheer fate, Pete and I had lunch on Monday with a former Rouse Company colleague, who was working for the Trammell Crow family. Pete brought up the Merritt opportunity. By Wednesday, the Trammell Crow people were in Baltimore, offering to do a joint venture with Merritt to repurchase the AT&T property. Merritt exercised his right of first refusal (the bank was not happy) and did the joint venture with Trammell Crow. Pete and I received a nice brokerage fee for arranging the venture. This was a great risk-reducer for Linden, and a feel-good story to help a friend (and stick it to the bank).

The mortgage brokerage business continued to provide a nice cash flow, but the passion and itch to return to real estate development nagged incessantly.

Several years later, the time would come to test the real estate development waters. Would Merritt be willing to sell one of the AT&T parcels? His response was that when we both had to do the workout deal with the bank, we stepped right up, and when he had the opportunity to buy back the property, we were there with the capital. Of course, they would sell a parcel, but maybe not their best one. They commented that it may take longer to put the deal together. We agreed on a parcel with a reasonable price. They were right. It took a lot longer to put the deal together, but eventually, we built an eighty-thousand-square-foot office and retail building, Lakeside. The timing could not have been better. The land cost was affordable. As the only new project in the market, the construction costs were favorable, and the project leased into a rising retail and office rental market.

One of the unique but overlooked aspects of the Lakeside site was that it fronted on two streets. Dobbin Road was a premiere retail address, and Stanford Boulevard was one of the best office addresses. Although a small site calls for one building, what if you could build a building with two fronts: retail and office? We drew the plans, and the CBRE office and retail brokers moved the building plans around on the site plan until everyone was satisfied that both uses would work.

The retail market in Columbia has long had strong demand and limited supply. This was especially true for smaller retailers. The Lakeside retail was specifically designed for the small guy. It leased up quickly. The office space had no new building competition. The office tenants were two Fortune 100 companies, the federal government, and a wealth management company. The Return on Cost was an unbelievable 17 percent. Merritt was also pleased, as the office rents in their buildings went up $1.50 per square foot with the arrival of walkable retail in Columbia Corporate Park.

The project became a cash cow. Along with Bel Air Town Center, it created the financial cushion that enabled Linden to grow as a real estate development company. Staying true to the Toombs Rule of Real Estate and product differentiation, it was time to look for larger mixed-use sites. WHY NOT ME.

The search led to the Horse Farm and Arundel Mills Corporate Park. Both fit the mold, mixed-use with about 300,000 square feet of office plus related retail. Both had unleveraged returns on costs above the 12 percent threshold.

At some point, the financial markets became swamped with money. Underwriting went wild. Lenders quoted unbelievable loans. The competition in the mortgage banking world was fierce, as fees plummeted and competitors lowballed their quotes to get business. Linden Associates left the market. The hope was that the existing real estate portfolio could comfortably carry the company alone. That proved to be the case.

LEARNING TO SAY NO

It is hard to say no to an opportunity when in a high-growth mode. A friend once described an entrepreneur as a "deal-seeking missile," which is true. A necessary part of a business strategy is sticking to the plan and living within the guardrails. McGill developed an unsuccessful shopping center by ignoring the guardrails. Linden Associates almost did the same thing, saved only by the advice of several friends and the all-important gut feeling.

PEARL OF WISDOM:
Trust your gut.

All the projects to date had been in the Baltimore suburbs. Opportunities came up north of town and in Annapolis, but nothing went far enough to become real. Baltimore City would issue Request for Proposals (RFPs) requiring urban development skills, not a match for us. One day, a ULI colleague suggested lunch to discuss a big project that the company she worked for had been awarded. She was the project manager. It was an interesting lunch and a very interesting project. Linden had seen the RFP several years earlier and had simply not seen the vision of the winning company.

I called several days later, wondering why she'd made the invite. Would Linden Associates, Inc. be interested in developing the project? The company she worked for was in deep financial trouble. The venture partner, the State of Maryland, had told her that if her company filed for bankruptcy, they would rebid the project to others. On the other hand, if her company sold its interest in the venture to a qualified developer, the venture could continue.

There was this one-inch-thick book on the project filled with economic spreadsheets. Going through the book was impossible even for an analytics geek. Several things stood out: The state owned this twenty-eight-acre, fully developed site. Back in the 1950s, the state had assembled the site and built numerous office buildings for the state's use. The buildings were in sad shape. The selected developer would create a mixed-use plan, build new buildings, and lease them to the state. The state would ground lease the building sites to the developer, as they developed with a base rent of $1 plus a percentage of the building cash flow. At the end of the seventy-year ground lease, the building ownership would revert to the state. The state would also build any required parking at their cost.

Forget the business analytics, spreadsheets, and economics in the book. Free land, free parking, 100 percent leased to the State of Maryland at market rents! The economics just had to work. What was I missing? So, I asked the WHY NOT ME question, more of a Why Me question. This was a different animal. Some of my business skills would still apply, but building a billion-dollar mixed-use project in an urban environment with the state government as your partner was all new. What about the project manager? Part of the proposed deal was that she be a partner in the new deal. Were there weaknesses not previously exposed that could tank the deal?

The carrots of free land, free parking, and state leases carried the day. Jump in, but be wary.

Several years earlier, Linden had tried to do a mixed-use project on a parking lot at a state-owned commuter rail stop. The state liked the deal, but the site restrictions proved insurmountable. The person at the Maryland Department of Transportation, who worked on the commuter rail stop, was now running this project. He supported our takeover of the developer role. We had sufficient experience and liquidity. The state approved our involvement.

We worked out a deal with the troubled developer, and the project headed for approval by the State Board of Estimates.

But something did not feel right about the deal. Our new partner became aggressive in wanting control of the partnership and being the lead developer. This was not what Linden Associates had signed up for. After long talks with Pete and others who have his people skills, we cut our losses. The company would remain in the deal, but have no further financial obligations. A compromise was worked out in the partnership agreement. This would enable the project to go forward. The state was made aware of the change and went along. The Board of Appeals approved the project and the first two occupancy leases.

As the current governor's term neared its end, things seemed to slow down. When the new governor came in, the project stopped completely. There never was a satisfactory explanation for what happened. The project ended up in the courts as the project team sought to be reimbursed for costs and lost profits.

PEARL OF WISDOM:
The lesson learned is that great economics do not necessarily make for a great project. If you have poor people skills, make sure there are skilled people around you with good advice. Their advice was to cut my losses and get out of the line of fire. Obey your guardrails. Stick

Christopher W. Kurz

*to the corporate strategy and culture. Advice
taken. It was fun to work on the project, and
the team had a world-class plan, but it was
not to be.*

WHY NOT US AT THE MACRO LEVEL: ATLANTA

As your business grows from the gleam in the eye where WHY
NOT ME is important, to the early years where WHY NOT US
is a driving force, your interest in your market makes WHY NOT
US applicable to your environs as well as your business. A successful company can only be so successful if its geographic location is not successful, and if its power brokers do not share a
WHY NOT US attitude.

Early in my career, I asked Alvin Ferst, Executive Vice President
of Rich's Department Stores in Atlanta, if he had an opinion on
the overbuilt Atlanta office market and its over 20 percent vacan-
cy rate. His answer spoke volumes. In his deep Southern accent,
Alvin said, "Chris, the office market is not overbuilt. It is just
under leased."

What most people saw as a problem, Alvin saw as an opportunity. Having excess office space would help grow Atlanta—a good
thing. This was symptomatic of the generally positive business
attitude in Atlanta at the time. It remains so today, and is prevalent
in most cities in the South. It is hard to find this attitude in the
Northeast.

PEARL OF WISDOM:
*With your successful business
comes a need and a responsi-
bility to actively participate in the economic
health of your town and region. It is not just*

a charitable act. At this point, your company needs a steady stream of top talent to grow. This talent has many options to live in other towns, like Atlanta or Austin. Building a WHY NOT US attitude in your town is good for you as well as everyone else.

So, what does this mean for your company's culture and business strategy? My view of the Japanese portrait still holds: Be aggressive, humble, relentless, and passionate. As you grow, think WHY NOT US for both the company and your town. Be true to your core strategies. Outside advisors and independent board members, looking at your strategies can give you excellent outside advice about evolving traits that may not be best for your enterprise.

The purpose of business is not the pursuit of the almighty dollar. It is a journey with like-minded people to improve the lives of your customers through your business. Enjoy the journey, maintain your work-life balance, and have fun.

CHAPTER 10
MEGA TRENDS: SUSTAINABILITY AND DIVERSITY, EQUITY, AND INCLUSION

Pay Attention

When your nose is to the grindstone, it is hard to lift your head, feel the breeze, and notice a fundamental change in the business landscape. If you train yourself to do so, great opportunities can emerge. To miss the change is not only a missed opportunity, but it could be detrimental to your success. Two such trends, one twenty-five years old and one fairly new, are worthy of your attention. They are sustainability and DEI: diversity, equity, and inclusion.

SUSTAINABILITY

Kermit the Frog says, "It's Hard Being Green." Kermit would know. He was green when nobody else was.

Advances in technology have become an increasingly important part of any business enterprise. Depending on the field, changes in technology can even be a monthly disruption. Commercial real estate as a business has historically not been impacted by technology. Accordingly, most people in the field are blind to any impact technology might have on their business.

In 2000, ULI headquarters called, asking that someone represent ULI at a symposium on sustainability. As the chair of the Baltimore ULI District Council at the time, I was asked to make an appearance at the symposium on Saturday morning. Usually, when there are real estate-oriented meetings in the Baltimore area, there are a bunch of business friends attending. At this meeting, there were no such friends. It was boring until Bill Browning from the Rocky Mountain Institute got up to talk. Bill told a story about a defense contractor with a building in California that the Rocky Mountain Institute helped convert into a green building. The motivation of the defense contractor was the anticipated savings in utility costs.

Once the improvements were made and the engineers moved back into the building, the defense contractor discovered that coffee consumption had gone through the roof. Intrigued by this, they soon discovered that people were finishing their projects early and hanging out around the coffee pot. Armed with this increase in labor productivity, their profit margins increased dramatically, and they were able to increase business without adding more labor. Eventually, word of this remarkable building leaked out. The Rocky Mountain Institute was contacted by a prominent business publication wanting to know about the building. RMI was delighted and passed on the contact information for the defense contractor to the magazine. Several weeks later, the business publication called RMI in a foul mood. They had contacted the defense contractor, whose response was that they neither confirmed nor denied the existence of the building. RMI called the contractor, wanting to know what the reluctance was to share this wonderful news. Their response was, "You've got to be kidding. This is a huge competitive advantage for us. Why do you think we would share it with anyone else?"

Bill went on to lay out the nuts and bolts for sustainable office development. It appeared, but had not been analytically confirmed, that people working in green buildings were approximately 15 percent more productive. The math goes like this. Usually, five people are working in any one-thousand-square-foot space at a labor cost of give or take $75,000 per person. That translated into a $375,000 per-year labor cost for the one thousand square feet. Fifteen percent of $375,000, the labor productivity savings from being in a green building, is $56,250 per year. Translated into real estate terminology, the savings are $56.25 per square foot per year. At that time, the market rent for office space was approximately $25 per square foot. The savings in labor costs were greater than the rent! If there were two buildings side by side, one green and one not, in a world of perfect information, and the owner of the regular building was giving the space away for free, tenants would still occupy the green building first because their effective rent was a negative $31.25 per square foot.

For a commercial real estate developer, this meant that building anything other than a green building was shortsighted. So, why were all commercial real estate developers not immediately changing over to green buildings?

There were three major problems with the acceptance of sustainable development. The first was that the real estate industry, as mentioned above, was oblivious to the impact of technology on the business. If no one was building green buildings, there would be no adverse impact. Think buggy whips around the year 1900.

The second problem was that the vocabulary of labor productivity, while standard in business, was not a part of the real estate vocabulary. If no one spoke the language, how could one communicate the benefits?

The third problem was that building green is complicated, and it was hard to quantify the specific benefits. To talk about sustainability was the equivalent of being a snake-oil salesperson.

The first opportunity to build a green building came with Arundel Mills Corporate Park. The architect, RTKL, was well-versed in sustainable design. One of their major contributions to the design of the building was the realization that, when a building component was made sustainable, the cost premium was partially offset by savings in other building areas.

For example, there are sustainable benefits to building a raised floor. The electrical and utilities run in an eight-inch space between the concrete slab and the elevated floor. In a conventional building, electrical and utilities are run in a thirty-six-inch space, called a plenum, between the ceiling and the slab above. RTKL's contribution was that the plenum was no longer needed with the raised floor, and the height of the building could be reduced by one foot per floor. Additionally, by running the heating, ventilating, and air-conditioning underneath the raised floor, as the air warmed up due to people and machines, it naturally flowed upward. In a conventional building, the air comes out of the ceiling. It must be pushed down into the space. The raised floor allowed for a much more efficient and healthier heating, ventilating, and air-conditioning system, with less tonnage and significant cost savings. When the building was completed, the "sustainability" premium for Linden Associates was less than 2 percent of construction costs.

Leasing the building as a green building proved to be more problematic. The traditional flow of information in leasing space is that the developer has her leasing broker, who talks with the leasing broker representing the prospective tenant, who talks with the tenant. The difficulty arises because while the developer and tenant may understand labor productivity, this was a foreign concept to the brokerage community. They had zero interest in discussing with their clients a concept they had never heard of nor understood. They would look dumb.

The creative solution was for our broker to get the name and phone number of the employee at the prospective tenant who had the profit and loss responsibility for the group going into the building. The developer, armed with this information, would call the tenant around 8:00 a.m. when the key employee was probably at work, but not surrounded by secretaries to intercept phone calls. The expectation was for the key employee to quickly lose interest after four or five minutes. The pitch about productivity took about three minutes and was generally effective. Once this 8:00 a.m. call had been made, I would call our leasing broker. Within two hours, our broker received a very irate call from the tenant broker.

"How dare you circumvent the process! How dare you introduce this foreign concept about labor productivity! Sounds like BS." This was a small price to pay for getting the building in the finals for consideration.

One day, our broker called to say that there was an important meeting later in the week, and attendance was required. Of course!

Upon showing up at the meeting, I asked, "Why are we here?"

His response was: "We're doing an intervention."

"Who?"

"You!"

"What? Why me?"

He and several other brokers at the meeting put it bluntly. These 8:00 a.m. phone calls were counterproductive and had to stop. The building had strong conventional attributes—floor plate size, location, and amenity base. The brokers could lease the building easily if I would just shut up and not talk about sustainability. They, of course, were right. I shut up, and the building leased up quickly.

> **PEARL OF WISDOM:**
> *It is possible to be ahead of technology and ahead of the market. A wise investment banker once said that the definition of a pioneer is someone lying along the side of the trail, dead. This pioneer, while well-intentioned, was not moving the wagon train, or the project, toward the promised land of being fully leased.*

The additional difficulty in building green was the difficulty in determining exactly what "green" meant. This problem was solved by the Green Building Council, which created a rating system called LEED, short for Leadership in Energy and Environmental Design. LEED removed the necessity to know the vocabulary, labor productivity, or the specifics of green design. LEED rated buildings on a not-so-complicated formula that gave points for green building features. The higher the point total, the greener the building. As LEED gained acceptance, tenants and leasing brokers relied on LEED ratings to determine an acceptable level of sustainability. No vocabulary is required—no snake-oil salespeople.

About this time, there was a call from one of our tenants, Cisco. The head of real estate was going to be in town and wanted to stop by to discuss interior space improvements to qualify their space for a LEED rating. We indicated that we had already drunk the Kool-Aid of sustainability and would be totally on board with changes to their space. He expressed appreciation and indicated that the impetus for these changes did not come from the Cisco real estate department, but came from human resources. When we asked why, he told this story.

Cisco, as with most other technology companies, is heavily reliant on continuously attracting the best talent. Accordingly, their human resources department tracks the percentage of accepted employment offers made to graduate and undergraduate technology students. Historically, Cisco hired approximately 95 percent of those offered employment. This number started to drop and caused great concern in the C-Suite. Was it a problem with pay? The human resources department researched the issue and said no, it was not an issue of compensation. The problem was that these students could choose where they wanted to work, and were seeking compatibility between their cultural values and those of their prospective employers. The bottom line was that Cisco was not perceived as a sustainable company. For Cisco to attract the employees they needed, Cisco had to become sustainable and not just talk the talk but "walk the walk." A part of walking the walk was being able to say that all their offices were sustainable and met high LEED criteria. Good to know, and a very good story to tell future tech company prospects. Much more credible than 8:00 a.m. phone calls.

DIVERSITY, EQUITY, AND INCLUSION

Sustainability is, in my opinion, the mother of DEI. How so? The Cisco executives learned a valuable lesson about attracting and retaining talent: It is (almost) never about the money. It was not only the people at the top of Cisco who learned this lesson, it was the next layer of management that absorbed this fact. They are the folks in charge twenty-five years later who remember their bosses almost making a big mistake. They will not make the same mistake.

Today's sustainability is DEI. Cultural priorities, like sustainability years ago, are very important today in recruiting and retaining talent. Look at the diversity on any world-class university campus. Have a meal at the student union and see how diverse the student body is. These venues were chosen by these smart students because of their learning opportunities and the cultural environment. It is not a long leap of faith to think that a similar work environment might be desired by the best and the brightest your company wants and must have.

Recently, a friend mentioned an interesting story from his town about a real estate brokerage firm that pitched an assignment they did not get. They circled back to the customer to find out why they lost and the others won. They were told both firms were equally capable and roughly the same in price.

As the other firm was leaving after their presentation, one of them mentioned that they had contributed to a "rights" march that weekend as a part of their general philanthropy. Not a big deal, but it spoke to their cultural values. That was the difference. The losing firm may have had great cultural values, but they were not on display.

PEARL OF WISDOM:
When your company makes a marketing pitch today, the people you bring from your company are as important as what you say. They reflect your unspoken cultural values and speak volumes to your customers. Make sure your customer is also aware of your corporate values.

Why is DEI controversial? It seems like a no-brainer to embrace

DEI. There is, however, a case to be made that DEI is an unnecessary intrusion into the business world. If your company meets these three criteria, then perhaps it may not fit. The three criteria are investment time horizon, labor and culture as a commodity, and a profit-only mentality. Think hedge fund or corporate raider.

If your time horizon is short, three to five years, it is likely that DEI will have a minimal impact on profitability. In these situations, the investor must deal with the cards they have been dealt with. They have no time to change the employee base and culture. Financial engineering is the tool of choice to rapidly improve corporate performance. The usual strategies are to sell off underperforming components like divisions or factories and add debt to repay investment equity.

In this short-term horizon, there is no time to hire a better labor force, or to tap their experience and expertise to improve profitability. You work with the existing labor force, viewing them as a commodity just like capital. Reduce the operating costs by laying off those who are not required for the short term. The assumption is that the poor performance of the acquired company is, in part, due to labor. Likewise, culture is a given, something that cannot be changed quickly. So, it is expendable.

Last, the sole goal of the investor is to increase profits, thereby increasing enterprise value and facilitating a favorable exit strategy. No need to think long-term, or build a culture and labor force that includes nonfinancial objectives. You can understand why high-profile business people in this line of work are campaigning to exclude DEI from inclusion in Wall Street's company evaluations or as a component of a pension fund's acquisition criteria.

The takeaway, possibly a Pearl of Wisdom—if you are not a hedge fund or corporate raider, ignore DEI at your own peril.

CHAPTER 11
SUCCESSION

The Queen is Dead. Long Live the King.

Succession comes in two forms: for the enterprise and for the entrepreneur.

THE ENTERPRISE

There are four ways to accomplish succession at the enterprise level: merging (also known as selling), going public, selling corporate assets, and dissolving the company (also known as closing the doors). This chapter will discuss merging and going public.

Rouse sold itself to a competitor. The competition to buy regional malls was fierce, and Rouse had decided it was unfeasible to buy at current returns. At a board meeting, one of the independent board members told management that if they were not the predator, they were the prey. Rather than wait for a predator to launch an attack, they went on the offensive, identified a suitable buyer, and consummated the sale of the company on an all-cash basis. The buyer did not choose wisely in capitalizing the acquisition and filed for bankruptcy several years later. The board director's observations were accurate, and management was astute enough to listen and act. Fortunately for Rouse shareholders, the transaction was all cash.

Alex. Brown & Sons was a venerable, successful investment banking firm in Baltimore. Among other areas of expertise, they were market leaders in identifying start-ups, helping them grow, and taking them public. As these companies grew, their capital needs increased.

When a company does a stock or bond offering, investment banking firms compete to underwrite and sell the offering. Part of this effort entails making a market in the customer's outstanding stock and debentures. In layman's terms, this means being the marketplace where the company's stock and bonds can be traded. The market maker often must have an inventory of stock or bonds on hand for future buyers. This requires large amounts of the firm's capital. Brown's problem was that, first as a partnership and then as a corporation, they did not have the capital base required to meet the needs of their growing customers. The customers eventually gravitated to larger firms with a larger capital base.

The lack of firm capital was even more frustrating because Alex. Brown could match wits and the ability to raise capital, with the big boys like Goldman Sachs and Solomon Brothers.

A local insurance company wanted to raise a large amount of money. Brown bid for the business and to be the lead underwriter on the offering. The insurance company told Brown they were not in the same league as the New York firms, but gave them a small allocation to sell. The rule was that you could not start selling until 8:00 a.m. on the appointed day. At 7:45 a.m., Brown called to say they had sold out their allotment. The insurance company was livid. Brown had broken the rule. Brown's response was that while it was 7:45 a.m. in Baltimore, it was already 1:00 p.m. in Paris. Brown bankers had gone to work at 3:00 a.m. Baltimore time and had sold their allotment in Europe! They got more of the offering to sell, but most importantly, they showed their local colleagues that Alex. Brown could swim with the big fish.

The ultimate solution for Alex. Brown was to merge with Bankers Trust. Bankers Trust was a big fish, large enough to do the larger stock and bond deals. The problem that arose several years later was that the Banker's Trust equity was only about 3 percent of its assets. When the next financial crunch came, they were on the ropes and sold to Deutsche Bank. The good news was that this was an all-cash transaction, and the Brown partners and share-holders were finally paid for their ownership.

The Columbia Bank had grown to a multibillion-dollar bank under the leadership of its cofounder, president, and CEO.

When it was time for him to step down, he sold the bank to a much larger, like-minded community bank. I was no longer a part of the bank leadership and not privy to why the board decided to sell. It does seem that most community banks sell when a leader-ship change is imminent.

Eventually, for these banks, the culture that made them successful is overtaken by the acquiring institution, and they become just another part of a regional or national bank. Part of the reason The Columbia Bank was successful was that, years earlier, there was another Columbia bank, Columbia Bank & Trust, owned by a Baltimore bank. At some point, the Baltimore bank did away with the CB&T name and folded them into the mother ship. Their unique place in the market went away, enabling us to take their place as the true hometown bank.

What these three organizations had in common was the humility to know their strengths and weaknesses. Perhaps they knew about

Jack's Pearl of Wisdom. They also knew when it was time to sell, and did so.

Going public can be a nice way to monetize value and keep the toys. Your organization may be in a field receptive to being public. When a privately held company needs to raise money, one option is to sell stock to the public and enable stock owners to buy and sell their stock in the stock market.

This is called an "initial public offering," or IPO. The Columbia Bank was a candidate to go public and did so as soon as profitable. The timing was not good. It had nothing to do with the bank or its financial numbers, and everything to do with the yin and yang of the IPO market for small banks. Start-up banks were a hot commodity when the bank was conceived. The founders did their homework and were successful in the initial capital raise. When leadership first thought seriously about going public, the small-bank market was still strong. Management made the decision to delay going public for one quarter to show continually improving financial results. During this quarter, the small-bank stock market cooled considerably.

Brokerage firms and investment banks invest in many different companies every day. Within the firm, various people are regarded as knowledgeable about particular business sectors. That person may not have the "analyst" title, but every broker knows to check in with her before investing in the sector. By the time the bank filed to go public, the small-bank market was soft, and the small-bank "analysts" gave lukewarm endorsements, positive enough to make the investment bankers happy, but not enough to cause stockbrokers to recommend the stock.

By that time, the bank had several hundred thousand dollars invested in going public and did not want to write off the effort.

Christopher W. Kurz

It was a slow go. Eventually, enough stock was sold, but at a lower price that didn't recover for several years.

> **PEARL OF WISDOM:**
> *One of the lessons learned was to understand why and when your stock would be attractive. For The Columbia Bank, it was two things. First, the timing was terrible. Should, or could, we have known? Probably not. Second, the compelling reason for buying the stock was the prospects for the future, not the current financial returns. Better investment banker advice would have helped.*

THE ENTREPRENEUR: COMING DOWN THE MOUNTAIN

At a national ULI meeting, a close friend gave a presentation on his company. Art was the third generation of company leadership. They had never sold a property. Art looked at the portfolio and determined that the portfolio should be pruned to eliminate obsolete, and otherwise marginally feasible, buildings.

The Rouse Company did something similar years earlier. As a student of their craft, Rouse commissioned a study of the future of retail. The study showed that high-end and discount retail would grow and gain market share at the expense of the middle market. Rouse rated all their malls A, B, C, or D. The A's, and the B's that could be elevated to A's, were kept. Everything else was sold, including several marquee malls that had been key to their past success. It was painful, but necessary.

This was a wake-up call for me. Our two wonderful children

had always been told to pursue their passion. Just as I did not do what my father did, they did not have to go into real estate. Their passions were not in real estate, and they chose not to join the company. Art's speech sent a clear message that it was time to turn the corner, assess the portfolio, and make plans for a future that may not involve me. In a sense, it was a WHY NOT ME moment, recalibrating and deciding to prune and scale back. Over the next six years, Lakeside, the eighty-thousand-square-foot cash cow in Columbia, and Bel Air Town Center, the shopping center northeast of Baltimore, were sold. The two newest twenty-acre mixed-use projects were kept with partners doing the day-to-day work.

Pruning a portfolio and selling off real estate requires an entirely different set of skills than developing. Being a deal-seeking missile, making things happen was not a viable exit strategy. The good news was that there was no urgency. An excellent and very patient retail broker guided us through a three-year process culminating in the sale of Bel Air. A partner bought the Lakeside partnership interest.

One of the curses of being a successful entrepreneur is that you love what you do so much that you just cannot stop. While the Linden Associates portfolio had been trimmed, a new set of opportunities emerged. Through ULI friendships came the opportunity to invest in real estate development projects being done by close friends across the country. This was not the result of a carefully thought-out plan. Instead, it was the serendipitous meeting with the chief investment officer of a family office who mentioned they were investing with a local apartment developer that we knew. A call to the developer indicated they raised a lot of their real estate capital from friends and family in affordable investment increments. After two such investments, I contacted other ULI friends in high-growth cities. They, too, raise friends

Christopher W. Kurz

and family money, and we have had the opportunity to invest in several projects.

In a way, the lack of interest in the family business was a blessing. No succession candidates, so no succession to plan or implement. So also was the nature of the business a blessing—assets that could be sold off one at a time at market value. Others have not been so lucky.

Most of the salient succession issues for the entrepreneur revolve around leadership (now and later), control (now and later), family, and enterprise valuation. A good way to think about succession in an entrepreneurial enterprise is to think of the founder as royalty.

"THE QUEEN IS DEAD, LONG LIVE THE KING."

In the majority of privately held, first-generation companies, the founder is the King or Queen. The Queen is accustomed to making the key decisions, no questions asked. Some Queens are benevolent and let senior leadership weigh in, but ultimately, the Queen makes the decision. Once you have been a Queen, it is very hard to no longer be a Queen. Perhaps that is why in Great Britain, the ruler is the King or Queen until they die. In the Ottoman Empire, when the Sultan died and his successor was identified, all other males in the household were killed. There was no question of who was now the Sultan.

The question is, "Who is the new Queen?" and "Have they been given sufficient power and control to govern?"

The challenge is to identify who has the competence and experience to lead. Large companies with boards of directors have procedures to identify such individuals and put them on course to succeed the incumbent. If the company is not doing well, this process can be truncated with a board member becoming the interim CEO while the board finds the new leader.

Large companies that are still controlled by an individual or family make for great drama film scripts as factions vie for influence and control.

For most companies, the question is whether a family member or existing senior employee should become the next leader. The faulty premise is that the anointed person wants the job. They often are interested, but lose interest when they see what the job entails. This is not unusual. In talking to business colleagues who have been through succession, it appears that up until the year 2000, the oldest, generally male, family member was the designated successor. They knew it and were expected to take the reins regardless of their interest. Since then, the shackles have loosened and the anointed member can say no.

This comes as an unwanted surprise to the current Queen, who is expecting Junior to fall in line. Now the Queen has to scramble to find a Plan B.

There are two givens in a good succession plan. The new Queen/King must have sufficient ownership control to run the enterprise without interference from others, and the old Queen/King has to step down (and away) when the new one takes over.

Ownership control means owning the majority of the company. Minority ownership, if any, must be entirely passive—no say whatsoever, and just along for the ride. Minority ownership may receive other family assets as a part of an estate plan, but not sufficient stock in the company to disrupt things, even if the new Queen/King is sending the company down the toilet.

A good friend went through succession planning for his company, designating the new King and setting a timetable for the transition. When that time came, he was not ready to step down. He balked and was thrown out of the company. He was no longer King. Good thing he was not in the Ottoman Empire or in feudal England. Another friend did the same process, gave the new ruler the necessary corporate control, and walked away when the new ruler took over. The company continued to survive, even thrive, under the new leadership.

CONCLUSION

The four main ingredients to a successful career as an entrepreneur are Passion, Attitude, Lifetime Learning, and the ability to benefit from Pearls of Wisdom passed down by others.

Your passion may be something that you have had as a child, or it might be something that evolves as you grow up. Passion is like love. You will know it when you see it, and once you see it, you cannot let go. My passion for commercial real estate sat well concealed until a random set of circumstances brought it to the surface. Would there have been other passions if the real estate had not happened? Maybe. Having had the good fortune to be passionate about something, it is hard to think of life without a passion. Such is the case for many people. May you be blessed to find a passion.

A question people often ask me is, why did my passion become commercial real estate? In retrospect, the profession lends itself to an entrepreneurial mindset. It is complicated enough so that the competition can be outwitted and outsmarted. Sometimes the competition does it to you. It was also easy to see into the future and identify what product characteristics would create product differentiation.

Last, there is a real sense that, in creating successfully built environments, you are helping the world become a better place. One of my proudest moments was meeting a woman in the park at Columbia Corporate Park (AT&T). Unprompted, she talked about how peaceful it was, and how it was an oasis for her immediately outside her office building. Her observations were a validation of all we had tried to create with this project.

Attitude. WNY NOT ME, US or YOU, was born out of necessity during my sophomore year in college. This process has worked quite well over the years. It is powerful to be able to have the structure to recalibrate what is going on and to make changes. You just need to be willing to act and step out of your comfort zone, aspiring for something you may not be sure you can find. Attitude requires confidence in your abilities. Being forced out of real estate did a major number on my confidence, and it took eight years to regain enough confidence to be a successful entrepreneur.

Pearls of Wisdom. They seem to happen randomly, and they probably do. There have likely been Pearls of Wisdom that went unnoticed and unappreciated, but the ones that were noticed and appreciated were foundational to success. Jack's observations about strengths and weaknesses, Scott Toombs's Rule of Real Estate, product differentiation, and Bill Rouse's comments in 1991 all made a huge difference.

As you think about your business career so far, there are Pearls of Wisdom that you might want to add to this book. Please write them down and think about them. They will help keep you grounded.

Not everyone benefits from a top-tier education or a first job like the one at Rouse. In my case, it became a linchpin to future success—a strength just like analytics and physical strength in the rowing shell. Not everyone has access to, or the opportunity for, such an education and first job. What you can control is your commitment to continuing your education and being a lifetime

Christopher W. Kurz

learner. Use it to fill the gaps in your education and training. Let it be a reality check and an opportunity to step outside the day-to-day, see your world from a different perspective, and learn from those who are wiser and smarter.

ACKNOWLEDGMENTS

This effort would still be between my ears had it not been for many amazing people.

It started with a comment to our daughter, Sarah, that I might write this book. The next day, one of my co-grandfathers, David Treadwell, called to say, "Sarah says you're thinking of writing a book. You need to do this. You have a story to tell." David is a journalist, author, and coach to aspiring authors. He knows the publishing industry, was an early reader (before the manuscript was proofed for spelling and grammar errors), and was a constant source of expertise and encouragement. Debbie, my wife; Tim, my son; Jim, my brother; and Candy, my sister, read early drafts with great comments.

I reached out to a real estate friend, John McNellis, who has written two books (and counting) for expert advice. Expecting a long email back about agents, editors, and publishing houses, the response was short:

"Hey Chris, here's my best advice. Reach out to Julie Trelstad and see what she has to say." I called Julie.

Julie Trelstad is an expert in navigating the book publishing world and an excellent coach in moving a "newbie" through the process. She came with the added benefit of having worked with John and also having started her career in the real estate world. She speaks real estate as well as publishing. Her observations changed the book from a memoir to a business guide for entrepreneurs.

On this journey, several authors gave sage advice on traversing the publishing gauntlet. Ambassador Rick Barton, and economists Leslie Lipshitz and Susan Shadler, each shared their experiences in publishing and marketing their books.

This book and its cover would not be so great without the experise of my sister, Candy Rogers. She is a graphic designer par excellence and patiently nursed this book to its present appearance.

In business, there have been many mentors at The Rouse Company, Maryland National Bank, HG Smithy, and Alex. Brown. Most of them are unfortunately no longer alive. My fifty-year membership in the Urban Land Institute produced many mentors and Pearls of Wisdom.

On the dark side of becoming an entrepreneur, Pete McGill greased the skids of my transition to the dark side and has been a great business partner and a good friend. Early in the days of the McGill Development Company, the head of real estate lending at Equitable Bank, Tom Frye took a liking to us and guided us through the banking maze. Our first accountant, Jim Cragg, told us that we should manage to cash flow, not taxes, and he would take care of the latter. Our lawyer, Neil Tabor, kept us focused and provided much-needed business advice, as well as his legal expertise.

APPENDIX

Real Estate Projects Developed by Linden Associates, Inc. and Its Predecessor Company

The following properties were or are being developed and owned in part by Christopher W. Kurz:

8989 Herrmann Drive, Columbia, MD

40,000 SF flex building built in 1983. Financed with UNUM. Sold interest in 1993.

Columbia Business Center, Columbia, MD

A 160,000 SF one story mixed-use project of office, flex and retail in a joint venture with Northwestern Mutual in 1985. The property featured a fitness center, heavily landscaped courtyards and commanded a $1.50 PSF rental premium. NML was bought out in 1987 and the project was financed with Aetna. Property interest sold in 1991 to partner, a REIT.

BWI Business Park, Dorsey, MD

A 40-acre mixed-use project of retail, office and flex. The property was sold to a Copley joint venture at a substantial profit prior to the start of construction.

Columbia Corporate Park, Columbia, MD

An 88-acre mid-rise office park planned for 1.5 million square feet and two hotels around a five-acre lake. Originally a joint venture with AT&T, the site was bought in partnership with a local industrial developer. Three buildings totaling 354,000 SF were built and a site was sold to Marriott who built a Courtyard hotel. Property interest sold to partner in 1992. A seven-acre site was reacquired in 1997 for the Lakeside Building.

Bel Air Town Center, Bel Air, MD

A 92,000 SF neighborhood shopping center. Built in 1990 and expanded in 1998 and 2001, the center features a Chili's, Taco Bell, and AAA. The center wqs substantially renovated in 2013 and sold in 2022.

Robert's Field Shopping Center, Hampstead, MD

A 90,000 SF neighborhood shopping center anchored by a Weis Food/Drug and a 9,000 Ace Hardware. Completed in 1991, the center was sold in 1994.

Lakeside Office and Retail Center, Columbia, MD

An 83,000 two story office and retail center leased to Cisco Systems, USA Digital, Gateway Computers, Social Security, Calico Corners and five restaurants. Opened in 1997, the center was financed in 2002 with J. P. Morgan for a ten-year term at 5.91%. Ownership interest sold in 2012.

Columbia Corporate Park 100, Columbia, MD

A 366,500 SF mixed use office/retail property developed on 20 acres starting in 2000. A joint venture with Merritt, the development rights were awarded in a competitive bid by the University of Maryland based on the proposed site plan. Site rezoned in one year. No opposition. First office building, 118,500 SF, and retail building (20,000 SF) completed in 2002. The remainder was completed by 2006.

Arundel Mills Corporate Park, Hanover, MD

A 400,000 SF mixed-use office/retail/hotel project developed on 20.2 acres across from Arundel Mills Mall. The hotel and day care sites were sold. Two 150,000 SF five story office and retail buildings were developed starting in early 2004. Project is completed with permanent financing on the two office buildings.

WHY NOT YOU!
The Entrepreneur's Playbook

CHRIS KURZ has co-founded a billion-dollar bank and started two real estate development companies. He has lectured at Harvard, Penn, local universities, and the Urban Land Institute, where he was a Trustee.

For more information on the book or the author, please visit www.WhyNotYou-Kurz.com.

For information on scheduling a book event or special discounts for bulk purchases, please contact us via email at cwkurz@linden-assoc.com or visit www.WhyNotYou-Kurz.com.

www.ingramcontent.com/pod-product-compliance
Lightning Source LLC
Chambersburg PA
CBHW031856200326
41597CB00012B/437